The Queen Has Good Bones

The History of Buffalo's Scrappy Resilience

Mark Donnelly, PhD.

RPSS PUBLISHING
Buffalo, New York

Copyright © 2026 by Mark Donnelly, PhD.

All rights reserved. No part of this publication may be reproduced, distributed,or transmitted in any form or by any means, including photocopying, recording, or other electronic or mechanical methods, without the prior written permission of the publisher, except in the case of brief quotations embodied in critical reviews and certain other non-commercial uses permitted by copyright law.

RPSS Publishing, Buffalo New York

429 Englewood Avenue, Kenmore, NY 14223

rpsspublishing.com

publisher@rockpapersafetyscissors.com

978-1-956688-69-6 Hardcover
The Queen Has Good Bones

Printed in the USA

RPSS PUBLISHING
Buffalo, New York

This Book is Dedicated to

"The Man in the Arena"

It is not the critic who counts; not the man who points out how the strong man stumbles, or where the doer of deeds could have done them better.

The credit belongs to the man who is actually in the arena, whose face is marred by dust and sweat and blood; who strives valiantly; who errs, who comes short again and again, because there is no effort without error and shortcoming; but who does actually strive to do the deeds; who knows great enthusiasms, the great devotions; who spends himself in a worthy cause; who at the best knows in the end the triumph of high achievement, and who at the worst, if he fails, at least fails while daring greatly, so that his place shall never be with those cold and timid souls who neither know victory nor defeat.

Someone who is heavily involved in a situation that requires courage, skill, or tenacity, as opposed to someone sitting on the sidelines and watching, is often referred to as "the man in the arena."

Theodore Roosevelt

"The Man in the Arena" is an excerpt from a speech delivered by Theodore Roosevelt, the 26th President of the United States, at the Sorbonne in Paris on April 23, 1910.

He could not have imagined that more than a century later, those words would serve as the dedication to this book. Yet they do. Because the speech distills something elemental: the stubborn courage of ordinary people who step into the arena, who accept dust and sweat as part of the bargain, and who keep pushing forward when easier options whisper their names.

It captures, with uncommon clarity, the grit and resilience of the men and women who keep our great city in motion.

Table of Contents

Introduction:
The Queen Doesn't Wave From a Balcony - 7

A Frontier Awaiting Its Fate -9

Times Beach
An Irish Waterfront Community, Lost and Reclaimed - 12

The War of 1812 – 14

Where Should the City Be?
Black Rock versus Buffalo and the Fight for the Erie Canal Terminus -16

A City Built With Scrappy DNA- 19

Grain Elevators
Monuments of Muscle and Concrete: Buffalo's Grain Elevators and the Scoopers Who Worked Them - 27

Remembering the Many Voices -30

A City That Chose a Side
Buffalo and the Abolitionist Movement -34

Forged for the Union:
Buffalo and the Crucible of the Civil War -36

Beer and Breweries in Buffalo
Grain, Malt, and the Long Pour – 38

The Railroads of Buffalo
Steel Tracks, Moving Grain, and a City in Motion -40

The Buffalo Fire Department
Flames, Brotherhood, and a City Built to Burn -42

The Buffalo Police Department
Order, Authority, and a City in Motion -44

Fire on the Waterfront
The Rise and Fall of Steelmaking in Buffalo -47

Pan-American Exposition of 1901
The City of Light and Its Shadows -49

A Sudden Oath in Borrowed Clothes
Theodore Roosevelt Becomes President in Buffalo-54

Albright-Knox Art Gallery
Buffalo's Modern Conscience -56

The Buffalo Colored Musicians Club
Where the Music Never Asked for Permission -61

Hand, Heart, and Hammer
The Roycroft Movement in East Aurora -62

Built to Move the World
Buffalo and the Legacy of the Automobile -66

The People's Palace
Buffalo Central Terminal -71

The Olmsted Park System
Buffalo's Green Blueprint -72

Buffalo's Built Environment
How Grain, Rails, and Money Quietly Summoned Architectural Giants to Buffalo -76

Kleinhans Music Hall
Modernism, Music, and a City That Listens -84

Forest Lawn Cemetery
Where Buffalo's History Comes to Rest -86

Between Silence and Survival
Buffalo's German Americans Through Two World Wars -88

Shadows at the Margins
T*he Ku Klux Klan in Buffalo* -90

The Queen Grew Wings -92

Forged in Weather and Will
A History of Sports in Buffalo -96

The Buffalo Broadway Market
A Living Immigrant Commons -100

The Rise, Fall, and Reinvention of Downtown Buffalo Retail -104

A Short History of Buffalo's Colleges -106

Curtain Up!
The Buffalo Theater District -111

The Buffalo Niagara Medical Campus
From Industrial Hinterland to Innovation District -114

When Buffalo Gathers
Festivals as Civic Ritual -116

The Buffalo & Erie County Naval Park
Steel, Sacrifice, and a Waterfront That Remembers -120

43North and the Spark of Buffalo's Startup Economy -124

The City That Shows Up -126

Canalside and the Outer Harbor
Full-Circle: The Future is Right Where it Began -131

What Endures -134

About the Author -136

The Queen Doesn't Wave From a Balcony

She stands.

Buffalo, the Queen City on the Lake, has never extended a manicured hand to recite accomplishments. She assumes you will notice the walls first. The brick is thick. The stone is unapologetically permanent. Buildings stand shoulder to shoulder as if conferring quietly about the next century. Nothing here feels temporary. That was intentional.

Buffalo was built by people who did not trust flimsy things, including promises, mild forecasts, or anyone who said, "This won't take long."

If cities had posture, Buffalo's would be a slight forward lean. Not theatrical. Ready.

Good bones are not about decoration. They are about structure. They are what remains when fashions fade and economies wander off chasing newer skylines. They are what let you renovate without collapse. Buffalo's bones were set early, when the Erie Canal bent west and decided this was where cargo would pause before braving Lake Erie. The city did not ask why history had tapped its shoulder. It asked how fast, how much, and who was on the next shift.

Opportunity arrived. Buffalo clocked it in.

That set the tone for a Queen who preferred usefulness over applause.

Here, the highest compliment was never "visionary." It was "solid." Solid did not flinch in February. Solid did not pack up when markets got restless. Solid held the line when the wind came sideways off the lake and made lesser plans reconsider themselves.

The people who built Buffalo carried that sensibility like a well-worn tool belt. They raised neighborhoods the way you raise children: practical, durable, with the quiet expectation that they would be tested. Churches were constructed with basements large enough to feed half a ward. Parks were drawn into the city's design because even workhorses require room to breathe. Grain elevators rose along the river in concrete cylinders so confident that modern architects would later point and call them prophetic.

Buffalo built heavy because Buffalo intended to remain.

In the Queen City, architecture does not merely decorate the past. It remembers it. You do not need a plaque when the building is still earning its keep. City Hall does not whisper. It declares. The towers along the Buffalo River do not court beauty. They command respect. Streets bear the names of people who were useful enough to shape something lasting, even if the stories have thinned with time.

Buffalo has never been sentimental about history. It has been loyal to it. Loyalty repairs. Sentimentality only frames.

When the system hummed, it hummed loudly. Whistles marked shifts. Freight clanked into place. Lunch pails knocked against calloused hands. The rhythm of the city was measured in labor and reliability. Work paid for homes, for church envelopes, for team jerseys and Sunday dinners. Tomorrow was expected to resemble today closely enough to plan around.

And then the pattern shifted.

The canals mattered less. The mills grew sparse. Highways cut new routes that did not always circle back. Efficiency was redefined somewhere else, in rooms where Buffalo did not have a seat. The Queen was not consulted about the rearranging of empires.

From the outside, this is where observers tend to misread the story. They speak of decline, as if Buffalo misplaced something delicate and irretrievable.

But good bones do not shatter when fashions change. They absorb stress. They redistribute weight.

The people noticed first. They always do. Extra shifts were taken. Kids were watched. Dollars were stretched with mathematical creativity. Kitchens became planning offices. Taverns functioned as dispatch centers. Parishes, block clubs, union halls, and living rooms carried responsibilities that never appeared in quarterly reports. When large systems retreated, small systems advanced, not dramatically, but dependably.

Buffalo grew quieter. Not emptier.

There were fewer grand pronouncements and more incremental adjustments. The Queen did not perform resilience. She practiced it. The difference is substantial.

Old structures were not erased out of embarrassment. They were repurposed out of respect. Elevators became landmarks. Factories became apartments. Waterfronts rediscovered their reflections. Institutions accepted second careers. Buffalo did not pretend the past had not happened. It assigned the past a new job description.

Reinvention here is rarely flashy. It is architectural. It works within load-bearing walls.

Through every cycle, the constant has been the people. Some never left. Some left and returned with sharper clarity. Some stayed long enough to become fixtures themselves, as steady as the facades behind them. They argued about sports, debated politics, critiqued the weather, and showed up anyway. Showing up remains Buffalo's most reliable industry.

The Queen City on the Lake does not require rediscovery. She requires recognition on her own terms.

Continuity matters here. Progress is measured in inches, not headlines. The most vital systems are human and demand maintenance, patience, and humor dry enough to survive a January wind off Erie. Reinvention in Buffalo does not erase identity. It layers it.

The Queen has good bones.

That is why she endures. That is why she adapts. That is why, when maps are redrawn and industries renamed, she remains upright, adjusting her stance rather than surrendering her ground.

Still standing where the water meets the city.

Still built heavy.

Still useful.

Still ready.

This book is about how those bones were formed, tested, and strengthened. It is about a city that never mistook hardship for finality. It is about the relentless reinvention of a Queen who does not boast, because she knows the structure will speak.

A Frontier Awaiting Its Fate

Long before surveyors drew lines on maps or engineers imagined a waterway to the West, the Buffalo River wound quietly through forests, wetlands, and marshes at the edge of Lake Erie. This was not an empty place awaiting discovery. For the Haudenosaunee Confederacy, and especially the Seneca Nation, the river was homeland and lifeline. Its bends held spawning fish, its banks nurtured corn, beans, and squash, and its waters carried memory. The Seneca name for the place, Tehoseroron, meant "where there is a place of the bass." It described relationship, not ownership.

A Sacred Place

Buffalo Creek was central to Seneca life. As the "Keepers of the Western Door," the Seneca guarded the eastern approaches of the Haudenosaunee world. Buffalo Creek was a place of settlement, ceremony, diplomacy, and sovereignty. Long before European arrival, it functioned as a node in a continental network of trade and communication. The land did not need improvement. It already worked.

First Europeans, First Disruptions

Europeans arrived by water. In 1678, French explorers under LaSalle navigated the lower Niagara River, portaging around the falls and establishing a short-lived settlement on Cayuga Island. There, they built Le Griffon, the first large ship to sail the upper Great Lakes. Preparing for that voyage, they landed near what later became Black Rock, using the river mouth as a staging ground. The buildings they erected near Buffalo Creek in 1758 were destroyed a year later when the French evacuated after the British captured Fort Niagara.

The first permanent European presence along Buffalo Creek came in 1758, when Chabert Joncaire built a house and barn and began trading with the Iroquois. His survival depended on diplomacy. Trade was not incidental; it was the only way to exist there.

British Rule and Indigenous Displacement

With the British victory in 1759, the Niagara Frontier fell under British control, remaining so until the Revolutionary War. The Seneca, allied with the British, paid a brutal price. In 1779, under orders from George Washington, General Sullivan led a scorched-earth campaign through the Genesee Valley, destroying Seneca villages and crops. Survivors fled westward toward British forts, eventually settling along Buffalo Creek in the spring of 1780. What had been homeland became refuge.

After the war, British control lingered. American settlement was restricted until the British evacuated Fort Niagara in 1796. In the meantime, the first non-Native settlers along the creek included Revolutionary War prisoners, traders, and interpreters. Captain William Johnston, a white interpreter trusted by the Seneca, was granted land near present-day Washington and Seneca Streets. Joseph "Black Joe" Hodges, a formerly enslaved man, and Cornelius Winney, a Dutch trader, opened a log cabin trading post in 1789 at the creek's mouth. Early Buffalo was multiracial, precarious, and dependent on Indigenous trade.

Land, Law, and the Holland Land Company

In 1791, financier Robert Morris purchased most of Western New York from Massachusetts

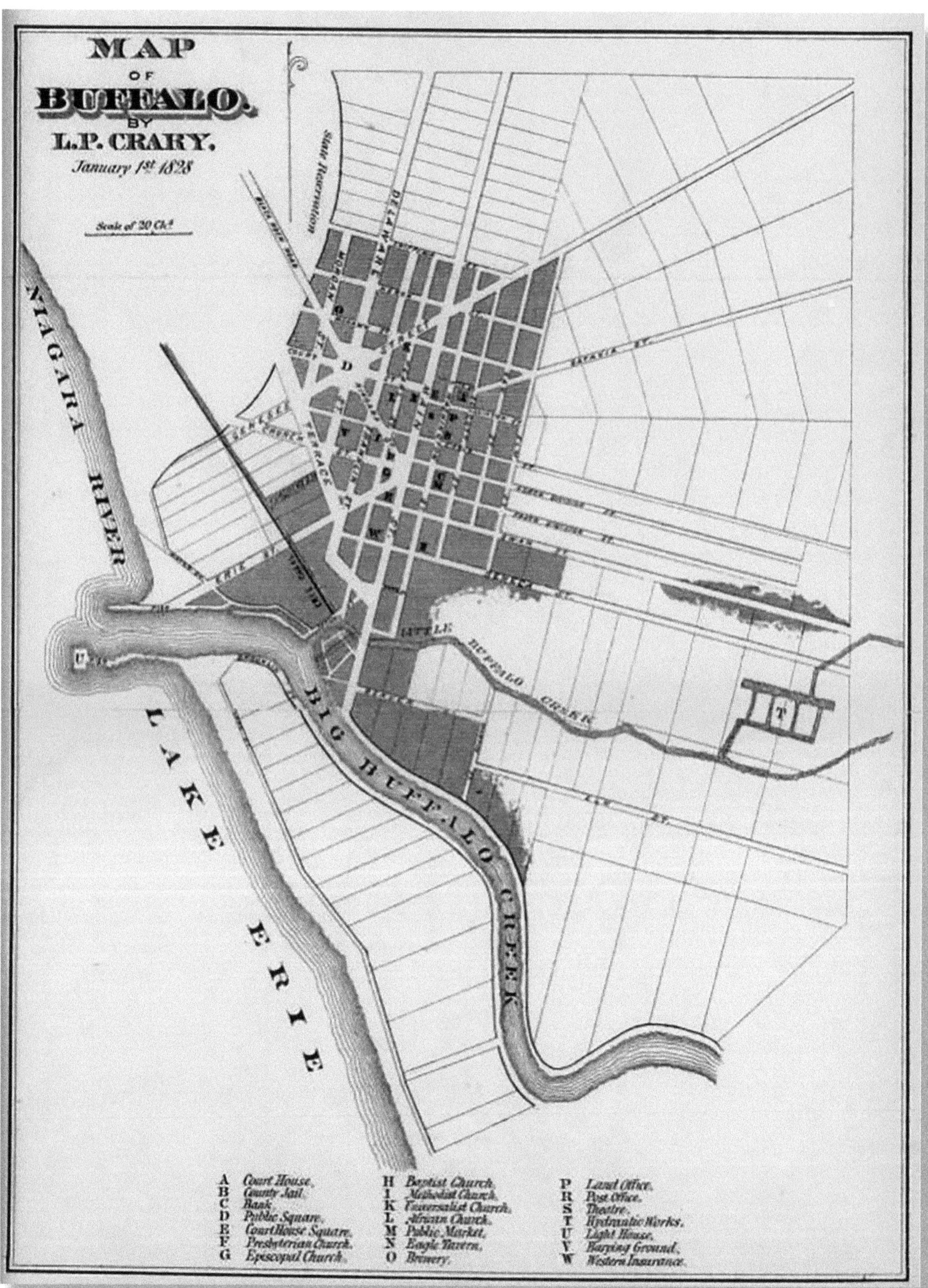
MAP
OF
BUFFALO.
BY
L.P. CRARY.
January 1st 1828
State Reservation
DELAWARE
NIAGARA RIVER
LAKE ERIE
BIG BUFFALO CREEK
LITTLE BUFFALO CREEK
TERRACE
A Court House.
B County Jail.
C Bank.
D Public Square.
E Court House Square.
F Presbyterian Church.
G Episcopal Church.
H Baptist Church.
I Methodist Church.
K Universalist Church.
L African Church.
M Public Market.
N Eagle Tavern.
O Brewery.
P Land Office.
R Post Office.
S Theatre.
T Hydraulic Works.
U Light House.
V Burying Ground.
W Western Insurance.

and quickly formed the Holland Land Company. The legality of the purchase remained uncertain due to existing Indigenous claims. That uncertainty was resolved in 1797 through coercive treaty negotiations along the Genesee River. With Seneca leader Red Jacket withdrawing in protest, the Haudenosaunee received $10,000 and three reservations along the Niagara Frontier. Buffalo Creek, once sovereign ground, was opened to American settlement.

The village that emerged was first called New Amsterdam, little more than an isolated outpost at the river mouth. Settlers lived by trading with Native communities, constantly alert to hostility bred not by proximity but by dispossession. Roads were few. The lake was difficult. Survival was provisional.

Drawing a City Into Being

In 1804, Joseph Ellicott arrived to impose order on uncertainty. Working for the Holland Land Company, Ellicott laid out a city plan based on Baroque principles, closely resembling Pierre L'Enfant's design for Washington, D.C. Broad radial avenues spread from public squares, anchored by what would become Niagara Square. Streets were named after Holland Land Company directors, signaling intention as much as geography. The plan assumed growth long before growth arrived.

Ellicott understood water. Exchange Street emerged as a commercial spine near the river. Residential districts clustered nearby, while forest still pressed close beyond Swan and Seneca Streets. The settlement clung to water because water was the only reliable connection to the world beyond.

War, Fire, and Rebuilding

Buffalo learned early that visibility carries risk. During the War of 1812, its position on the frontier made it a target. In December 1813, British forces burned the village nearly to the ground. Homes, businesses, and wharves vanished in a single night. The lesson was immediate and enduring: living here meant rebuilding.

Buffalo did not linger in mourning. It rebuilt without melodrama. Loss became information. Build sturdier. Organize faster. Assume interruption. This habit would define the city.

The Canal Changes Everything

The arrival of the Erie Canal in 1825 transformed Buffalo utterly. The canal did not just move goods; it redefined ownership, labor, and destiny. For the Haudenosaunee, its opening marked celebration elsewhere and loss here. For Buffalo, it meant becoming the western gateway to the American interior. Grain, people, and ambition poured through the harbor. A frontier outpost became the Queen City of the Lakes.

Remembering the Many Voices

Today, as kayakers paddle past restored grain elevators and walkers trace the boardwalks of Canalside, it is worth remembering that the Buffalo River is layered with stories. They are stories of the Haudenosaunee who named the waters, of Black laborers who loaded the docks, of women who kept households afloat, and of immigrants who reshaped a city. Buffalo's early history is not a straight line toward progress. It is a convergence of displacement and opportunity, violence and vision, water and will.

Buffalo did not choose to be important. It was drafted by geography, tested by war, and rebuilt by people who understood early that stability here was never guaranteed. The water kept connecting, carrying, waiting. And the city, born on its edge, learned to do the same.

Times Beach

An Irish Waterfront Community, Lost and Reclaimed

Nestled where the Buffalo River meets Lake Erie, Times Beach has lived many lives, but for much of its human history it was shaped by Irish hands and Irish necessity. Long before it became a nature preserve, this narrow stretch of shoreline functioned as a working-class refuge for families whose lives were bound to the water. Few places along Buffalo's waterfront reflect more clearly the arc of Irish immigrant experience: arrival, labor, displacement, and quiet erasure, followed much later by an unexpected return of meaning.

The origins of Times Beach lie in the early nineteenth century, when Buffalo's harbor was carved out of marsh and shifting sand. Breakwalls and dredging altered currents at the mouth of Buffalo Creek, creating a sandy spit that engineers had not fully intended but quickly exploited. What emerged was marginal land, unstable and overlooked, yet close to work. For Irish immigrants arriving in steady waves throughout the nineteenth century, that proximity mattered more than permanence.

By the late 1800s, the area known as Seawall Beach had become a dense Irish working-class settlement. Cottages were built cheaply and close together, expanded when wages allowed and repaired after storms demanded it. Taverns, boarding houses, and seafood shacks lined muddy paths rather than formal streets. Many residents were fishermen, dockworkers, grain scoopers, and laborers who loaded ships and shoveled grain by hand. Others ran small businesses that served the waterfront economy. Poverty was common, but so was pride. Life at the seawall was defined by work, kinship, and endurance.

The lake was both livelihood and threat. Flooding was routine. Sanitation was poor. Disease moved quickly through crowded housing. Yet the Irish families who lived there remembered the neighborhood as lively and close-knit. Children played along the water. Neighbors watched one another's doors. Survival depended less on institutions than on shared obligation. This was not an idyllic place, but it was home, built by people who had

already learned how to endure hardship.

By the early twentieth century, that informality became a target. City leaders increasingly viewed Seawall Beach as an embarrassment, a slum standing in the way of modern harbor plans and industrial efficiency. Reformers framed the neighborhood as unsanitary and disorderly, ignoring the economic forces that had driven its creation. In 1917, Buffalo launched a slum-clearance campaign that erased the Irish community almost entirely. Homes dating back to the 1840s were demolished. Taverns were shuttered. Hundreds of residents, known collectively as the "Beachers," were displaced with little compensation or support. The city made room for industry by removing the people who had made the waterfront function.

For the Irish families who had lived there, the loss was profound. What had been built over generations disappeared in months. Many relocated deeper into South Buffalo, carrying with them memories of the water and a sense of betrayal that lingered long after the buildings were gone.

For a brief moment, Times Beach seemed poised for reinvention. In 1931, the Buffalo Times proposed transforming the abandoned sand spit into a free municipal bathing beach. Lifeguards were stationed. Changing areas were installed. Crowds arrived on summer days, reclaiming the shoreline for leisure rather than labor. Health officials initially declared the water nearly as clean as a swimming pool. The site's name finally matched its purpose.

That promise collapsed quickly. Pollution from untreated sewage and industrial discharge overwhelmed the area. Water tests revealed coliform bacteria levels far beyond safe limits. Swimming was discouraged, then banned altogether by the mid-1930s. Once again, Times Beach was abandoned, its potential sacrificed to the same industrial priorities that had displaced its residents.

For decades afterward, the site served as a dumping ground for dredged material from shipping channels. Sediment piled up. Access was restricted. What had once been a living Irish neighborhood became a blank space on the map, shaped by labor but emptied of people. The voices, music, and daily rhythms of the seawall were gone.

And then, quietly, something unexpected happened. As shipping declined and dumping slowed, grasses began to grow. Wetlands formed. Birds returned. An accidental ecosystem emerged on land created by industry and abandonment. Instead of forcing development once again, Buffalo chose restraint. Times Beach was designated a nature preserve, allowing recovery rather than construction to define its future.

Today, visitors walk trails through tall grass where Irish cottages once stood. The lake stretches wide and indifferent beyond the breakwalls. Wind and water dominate where voices once carried. The transformation is not sentimental, but it is instructive. Times Beach now serves as a memorial without plaques, a place where absence tells its own story.

For Buffalo's Irish community, Times Beach stands as a reminder of both endurance and dispossession. It reflects how immigrant labor built the waterfront, how immigrant neighborhoods were erased when they no longer fit civic ambitions, and how memory can survive even when structures do not. In allowing the land to recover rather than be remade yet again, Buffalo has unintentionally honored the people who once lived there.

Times Beach asks the city to remember that not all progress is linear, and not all losses are meant to be forgotten. Sometimes the most honest way to honor a community is to leave space for reflection, and let the land carry the story forward in silence.

The War of 1812

When the War of 1812 reached the Niagara Frontier, Buffalo was not yet a city in any modern sense. It was a raw lakeside settlement, a hinge between wilderness and ambition, where taverns, docks, warehouses, and rough-hewn homes clustered along muddy streets. Its location, however, made it unavoidable. Sitting at the eastern end of Lake Erie, opposite British-controlled Upper Canada, Buffalo became both a strategic asset and a target. The war would burn the village nearly to the ground and permanently shape its character.

The conflict between the United States and Great Britain began in June 1812, fueled by maritime disputes, trade restrictions, and unresolved tensions from the American Revolution. On the Niagara Frontier, the war was immediate and intimate. The Niagara River was not an abstract boundary but a visible, crossable line. Cannon fire echoed across the water. Smoke rose on both shores. Buffalo lived within sight and sound of the conflict.

Even before hostilities began, Buffalo mattered because of logistics. It served as a transfer point between lake traffic and overland routes. Once the war started, that role intensified. Buffalo became a staging ground for American troops, supplies, and repeated invasion attempts aimed at Canada. Soldiers moved through in steady waves. Boats crowded the harbor. Warehouses filled with food, ammunition, and equipment. The village became a military corridor, exposed to the consequences of strategic decisions made far away.

American leaders believed Canada could be taken quickly, forcing Britain to negotiate. That confidence proved misplaced. Campaigns were poorly coordinated, militia units were undertrained, and leadership shifted uncertainly. British forces, Canadian militia, and Indigenous allies defended Upper Canada effectively. Buffalo, lightly defended and highly visible, paid the price for those failures.

The turning point came in December 1813. Earlier that month, American forces burned the Canadian town of Newark, now Niagara-on-the-Lake, forcing civilians into winter conditions without shelter. The act shocked observers and demanded retaliation. That retaliation came swiftly.

On the night of December 30, 1813, British forces crossed the Niagara River near present-day Fort Erie. They overwhelmed American defenses at Black Rock and advanced south toward Buffalo. What followed, often called the Battle of Buffalo, was less a traditional engagement than a collapse. American militia broke under pressure. British regulars, supported by Indigenous warriors, advanced methodically. By morning, Buffalo was defenseless.

The destruction was nearly total. British troops burned almost every structure in the village. Homes, barns, warehouses, taverns, and stores were reduced to ashes. Only a handful of buildings survived, spared by chance rather than intent. Residents fled into the freezing night, carrying what little they could. In a matter of hours, Buffalo went from supply hub to smoking ruin.

Nearby Black Rock suffered a similar fate. Mills and docks were destroyed, crippling what little infrastructure existed along the river. The message was clear: the Niagara Frontier was a

theater of total war, where civilian settlements were legitimate targets.

The burning of Buffalo shocked the young nation. Newspapers reported on civilian suffering and material loss. Locally, the trauma was immediate. Families were left homeless in midwinter. Livelihoods vanished overnight. Yet even amid devastation, a stubborn resolve emerged.

Fighting continued into 1814, including major battles at Chippewa and Lundy's Lane. Though those engagements took place in Canada, Buffalo remained a critical rear area, slowly rebuilding while war still raged. Troops marched past blackened foundations and temporary shelters.

Indigenous nations played central roles throughout the conflict, often overlooked later. Leaders such as Red Jacket navigated dangerous political terrain as imperial powers clashed around them. For many Indigenous communities, the war proved catastrophic regardless of allegiance.

When the Treaty of Ghent ended the war in December 1814, Buffalo emerged battered but unbroken. Nearly everything tangible had been lost. What remained was resolve. Rebuilding began immediately. Streets were reestablished. Trade resumed. Destruction and renewal became foundational experiences.

The War of 1812 was Buffalo's violent initiation. Fire tested its foundations. Loss sharpened its ambition. Long before canals, elevators, and mills defined the skyline, Buffalo learned a defining lesson in 1813: survival here would require resilience.

Where Should the City Be?

Black Rock versus Buffalo and the Fight for the Erie Canal Terminus

At the dawn of the nineteenth century, the future of Western New York hinged on a single, deceptively simple question: Where will the Erie Canal connect to Lake Erie? The answer would determine not only the canal's success, but which small frontier settlement would become the gateway to the West. A fierce rivalry emerged between two villages separated by just three miles of forest and ambition: Buffalo and Black Rock.

Today, Black Rock is a Buffalo neighborhood. In the early 1800s, it was a separate and arguably stronger contender. The canal prize promised immense financial potential. Whoever won would control the transfer point between inland waters and the Great Lakes, a commercial choke point destined to shape the national economy.

Geography as Destiny

Lake Erie posed an immediate challenge. Unlike other Great Lakes, its eastern shore offered no natural deep-water harbors. Both Buffalo and Black Rock lay near the lake's northeastern corner, south of the Deep Cut at Pendleton, making them the most plausible candidates.

Buffalo, however, was unimpressive at first glance. With fewer than 2,000 residents, it was little more than a quiet stopover for westward travelers. Despite its lakeside location, it lacked a harbor entirely. Strong offshore currents, shallow waters, and a stubborn sandbar made docking nearly impossible. On paper, Buffalo looked like an unlikely choice.

Black Rock, by contrast, appeared ready-made. Named for a one-hundred-foot outcropping of dark stone that formed a natural wharf, the village sat just upstream on the Niagara River. Sheltered by Bird Island and Squaw Island, Black Rock had a functional harbor and a busier settlement. The river connected directly to Lake Ontario, offering an established trade route. To many observers, Black Rock seemed the obvious terminus.

Yet that river was also Black Rock's Achilles' heel. The Niagara River's current was so strong that sailing vessels struggled to move upstream into Lake Erie. Enter Sheldon Thompson, a local entrepreneur who devised a solution known as the "horn breeze." With a team of fourteen oxen, Thompson hauled boats upriver against the current. Ingenious, but hardly scalable for a canal intended to move the commerce of a continent.

Champions and Interests

Black Rock's most influential advocate was Peter Porter, a politician, soldier, lawyer, and savvy businessman. Porter had significant financial interests tied to Niagara River navigation. His company already portaged boats around Niagara Falls, thirty miles north, enabling travel between Lake Ontario and Lake Erie. If the canal ended at Black Rock, Porter's enterprises would flourish.

Buffalo, meanwhile, had fewer natural advantages but growing political momentum. In

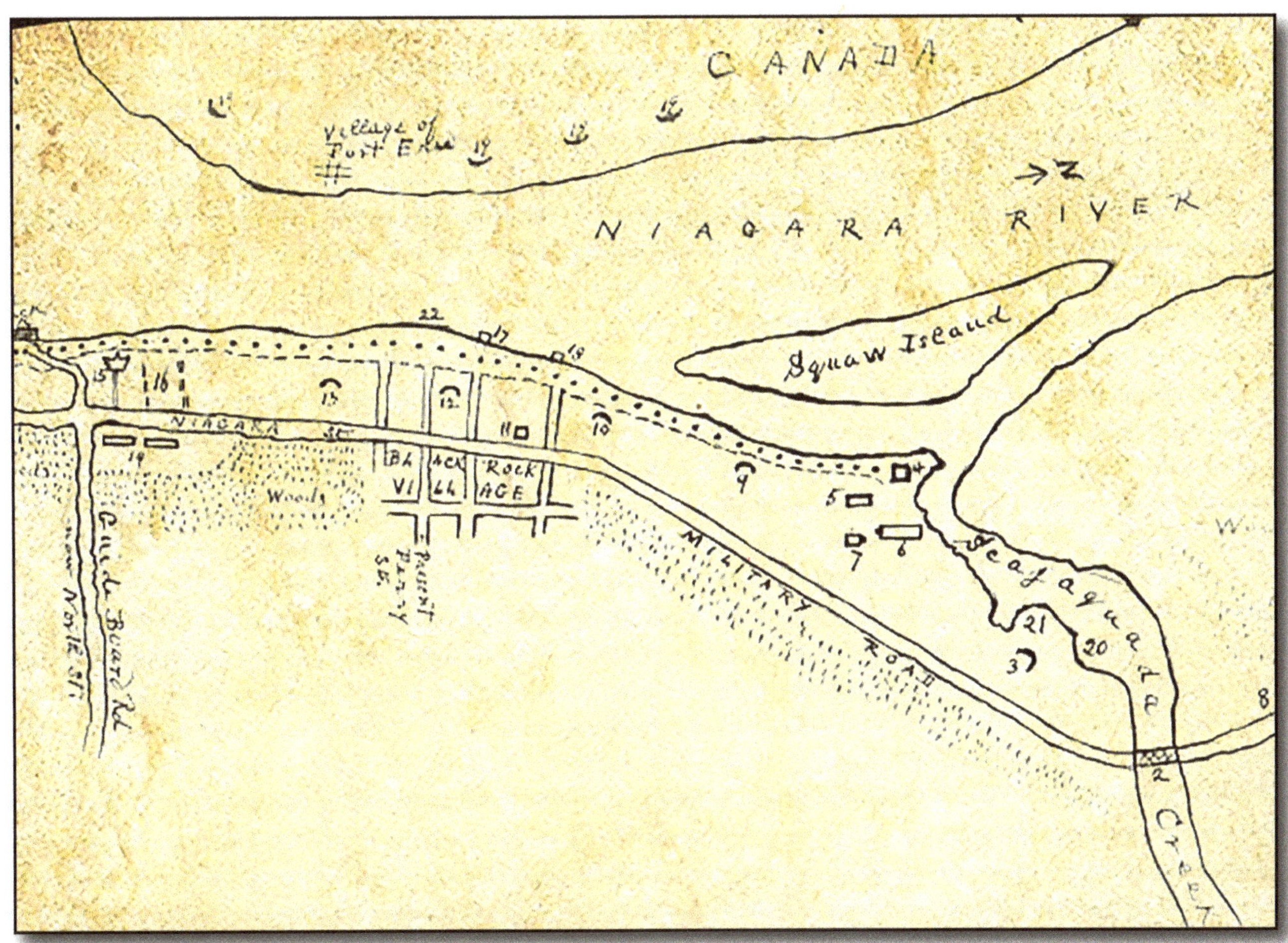

Early map of Black Rock

1816, a meeting was held to discuss creating a harbor at Buffalo, and the Canal Commissioners tentatively selected it as the terminus. DeWitt Clinton, the canal's greatest champion, famously predicted that Buffalo would one day rival New York City in power and importance. The remark enraged Black Rock's backers.

Engineering, Influence, and Reversals

The debate refused to settle. In 1818, Clinton asked engineer William Peacock to re-survey the sites. Peacock, a close friend of Joseph Ellicott, who had laid out Buffalo's street plan, delivered a decisive report in 1819. Buffalo, he argued, was "the key" to a vast inland navigation system stretching more than 2,000 miles, provided a massive pier was built extending a thousand feet into Lake Erie south of Buffalo Creek.

Buffalo moved quickly. Its backers secured a $12,000 state loan on April 7, 1819, the same day the legislature authorized construction of the canal's western division. The debt would be forgiven if the canal ended at Buffalo, a gamble that turned the loan into a de facto wager on destiny. Unfortunately, the Panic of 1819 made financing precarious. Buffalo faced a cruel paradox: without a harbor, it would never get the canal; without the canal, the harbor was useless.

Meanwhile, Black Rock pressed its case. Porter launched the Walk-in-the-Water, the first steamboat on Lake Erie, in August 1818. Hauled upriver by oxen and steaming to Detroit and back, the vessel proved Black Rock's operational viability. Investors from Albany and New York City took notice.

Chief Engineer David Thomas arrived in 1819 to make a final recommendation. Courted aggressively by both sides, Thomas ultimately chose Buffalo. Improving Black Rock, he concluded, would be prohibitively expensive, and lake winds would impede navigation. His report should have ended the matter. It did not.

Chaos Before Certainty

Buffalo began harbor construction in 1820 under brutal conditions, guided by relentless lobbying from Samuel Wilkeson. Yet reversals continued. In 1821, engineers James Geddes and Nathan Roberts recommended Black Rock. Six months later, Thomas returned with Canvass White and Benjamin Wright and reversed course again, endorsing Buffalo. Geddes refused to sign the report in protest.

Fate intervened dramatically when a storm destroyed the Walk-in-the-Water. Its engines were salvaged and rebuilt in Buffalo, a symbolic blow to Black Rock's cause.

The final showdown came in June 1822, when canal commissioners and engineers convened in Buffalo. Porter presented plans for a Niagara River harbor. Wilkeson told stories of battling storms and stubborn sandbars to create Buffalo Harbor. Buffalo prevailed again. Still, uncertainty lingered until a decisive move: construction of an "independent canal" section running parallel to the Niagara River, bypassing Black Rock entirely.

Victory and Consequence

In the spring of 1825, the matter was settled. The Erie Canal officially terminated at Buffalo. Black Rock's experimental harbor washed away in a flood in May 1826, sealing its fate. The canal's success ignited Buffalo's meteoric rise and hastened Black Rock's decline. In 1853, Black Rock was annexed into Buffalo, its rivalry resolved not by compromise, but by absorption.

The battle between Black Rock and Buffalo was more than local squabbling. It was a collision of geography, engineering, politics, and personality. Buffalo won not because it was ready, but because it was willing to be remade. In choosing Buffalo, the canal commissioners did not merely select a terminus. They chose the city that would become the Queen City of the Lakes.

Mildred C. Green, 1825 Village of Black Rock

A City Built With Scrappy DNA

Buffalo was never meant to be gentle.

From its earliest days, this place demanded something extra from the people who chose it. Extra stamina. Extra stubbornness. Extra nerve. The land itself was a negotiation. Marshy ground, violent weather, contested borders, and the constant sense that history could turn hostile overnight. Buffalo did not reward delicacy. It rewarded resilience.

That trait did not emerge later as civic mythology. It was baked in at the start.

The city's founding figures were not polished visionaries operating from a safe distance. They were improvisers, risk-takers, and occasionally troublemakers who blurred lines between professions and principles. They governed by necessity. They defended with whatever was at hand. They argued, rebuilt, and pushed forward even when the odds suggested retreat.

Joseph Ellicott. Samuel Wilkeson. DeWitt Clinton. Cyrenius Chapin. And later, Bishop James Quigley. Each played a part in Buffalo's formation, whether by pen or plow, compass or cannon, law or labor solidarity. Together, they forged a civic DNA that still shows itself whenever the city is counted out and refuses to comply.

Joseph Ellicott:

Drawing a City Into Being

Joseph Ellicott arrived before Buffalo had any right to confidence. The settlement was small, muddy, and uncertain of its future. What Ellicott brought was not just surveying equipment, but audacity.

Working for the Holland Land Company, Ellicott laid out a street plan that assumed success long before success was guaranteed. Broad radial avenues. Public squares. A geometry that suggested a city of importance, not a frontier outpost hedging its bets. He was, in effect, drawing a future and daring reality to catch up.

This mattered more than aesthetics. Cities grow into their plans. Ellicott's Buffalo was designed to handle scale, commerce, and movement. It assumed people would come. That goods would flow. That the settlement would matter. In a young nation still defining itself, this was a bold act of belief.

Ellicott did not stop at maps. He promoted Buffalo relentlessly, invested personally, and pushed infrastructure improvements. He understood that cities do not happen by accident. They are argued into existence through persistence and persuasion.

Buffalo's tendency to think big before it is ready can be traced directly to Ellicott's influence. The city learned early that ambition could be a tool, not a liability.

Cyrenius Chapin:
Healer, Fighter, Rogue

If Ellicott gave Buffalo its form, Cyrenius Chapin gave it nerve.

Chapin was a physician by training, but the frontier had little use for single-purpose men. He became a judge, a civic leader, and when circumstances demanded, a militia officer. He blurred lines comfortably. He healed and he fought. He enforced law and broke convention. He embodied the messy pragmatism of an early American border town.

Chapin was a proud Freemason, a rare Federalist who broke with his party to support the War of 1812, and a man infamous for his fondness for strong drink, colorful profanity, and reckless daring.

A Frontier Doctor Turned Raider

Born in 1769, Chapin practiced medicine in Buffalo for a decade before deciding that war offered more thrills than the sickroom. At 44, he took command of the mounted volunteers recruited at Buffalo. Their raids across the Niagara River were bold, destructive, and often lucrative, earning them the nickname "the Forty Thieves." For Chapin, the war was both patriotic duty and personal adventure.

Beaver Dams: Captor Becomes Captor

In June 1813, Chapin and 28 of his men were captured during the Battle of Beaver Dams. Escorted toward Kingston by boat under a guard of 16 British soldiers, Chapin bided his time. When the guards stopped to drink grog, he struck. The Americans overpowered them, seized the vessel, and forced their astonished captors into captivity.

There was, however, one problem: Chapin didn't know how to sail. His triumphant return turned slapstick when he ran the captured boat hard onto the rocks near Fort George. Chapin marched in, his own captors now his prisoners.

Burning of Buffalo

Dr. Chapin was not polished. He was effective. That effectiveness was tested brutally on December 30, 1813.

British regulars and their Native allies descended on Buffalo with overwhelming force. The town's defenses were laughably inadequate. Supplies were scarce. Weapons were mismatched. Morale was fragile. Chapin rallied what defenders he could, including a militia armed with little more than determination and improvisation.

At one point, the defenders attempted to use a decrepit cannon barrel strapped to a wagon. It managed a single blast before collapsing into useless fragments. It was almost farcical. Almost.

But that one blast mattered.

Outnumbered and outgunned, the defenders could not hold. But their resistance delayed the British advance long enough for hundreds of civilians to flee. As the militia finally broke and ran, Chapin reportedly shouted words that would echo through Buffalo's legend:

"Every man for himself & the Devil for us all!"

It was not a speech crafted for posterity. It was a raw acknowledgment of reality. Survival over ceremony.

The British torched Buffalo, reducing it to ashes. Homes, businesses, and institutions were wiped out. Many towns would have ended there.

He stayed. He tended the wounded. He comforted survivors. He urged rebuilding. He helped reestablish civic order when despair would have been understandable.

After the war, Chapin rebuilt his medical office and house on its original foundation. He resumed practicing medicine, helped establish the Erie County Medical Society, and promoted agriculture through the local farming society. He died in 1838, remembered as Buffalo's "warrior-doctor"–the man who stood when standing seemed impossible.

Samuel Wilkeson:
The Art of Starting Over

Samuel Wilkeson knew loss intimately.

A merchant and landowner, Wilkeson had invested heavily in Buffalo's early promise. When the British burned the town, he lost nearly everything. Property. Infrastructure. Security. The rational response would have been to walk away.

Wilkeson chose the opposite.

He became one of Buffalo's fiercest advocates for rebuilding and expansion. He pushed harbor improvements, better navigation, and infrastructure that would make Buffalo indispensable to regional trade. He understood that Buffalo's geography was not a liability but a hinge. A transfer point where movement paused, shifted, and resumed.

That pause was opportunity.

Wilkeson lobbied, invested, lost, and rebuilt repeatedly. His life reads like a rehearsal for Buffalo's later industrial cycles. Boom. Bust. Reinvention. He believed that disruption could be turned into leverage if the city committed fully.

Buffalo's instinct to find opportunity inside upheaval is Wilkeson's inheritance.

A Blind Mule, and the Making of Buffalo Harbor

In one of the most enduring and telling stories from Buffalo's early history, Buffalo's harbor was not built by inevitability. It was built by stubbornness.

At the center of that stubbornness stood Samuel Wilkeson, a man whose biography reads less like civic planning and more like an endurance test. Wilkeson believed, with near-religious intensity, that Buffalo's future depended on its harbor. Without one, the settlement was just another wind-scoured outpost on Lake Erie. With one, it could become indispensable.

The problem was that nature was not cooperative.

Lake Erie was shallow, violent, and unpredictable. Sandbars migrated. Storms erased progress overnight. Federal support was thin. Engineering expertise was scarce. Many doubted that Buffalo's shoreline could ever support a reliable port at all.

Wilkeson did not have an engineering degree. What he had was observation and audacity.

Watching currents and storms, he proposed a radical idea for the time: build piers that would guide the lake's natural flow, forcing the current to scour a deeper channel rather than fight it. It was not textbook engineering. It was practical, empirical thinking. Work with the water instead of against it.

In 1820, Wilkeson put his own money and muscle behind the idea. He did not wait for full approval or perfect funding. He rallied townsmen, drove piles, dredged channels, and hauled stone. He worked in mud up to his knees, often shoulder to shoulder with laborers, leading by example. Wilkeson personally oversaw harbor construction using the tools and labor available to him. Among those tools was a mule. Not a strong, prime animal, but a blind mule. A half-broken creature tasked with hauling stone and equipment through mud and water to build breakwaters that would almost certainly be damaged by the next storm.

The image is almost too precise.

A blind mule, plodding forward without seeing the result. A man convinced the effort mattered even when success was invisible. Together, they pushed stone into place and refused to be discouraged by setbacks that would have stopped a more cautious planner.

Storms destroyed early work. Money ran out. Critics scoffed. Wilkeson rebuilt anyway.

Slowly, against long odds, the harbor began to take form. The piers altered the current. The channel deepened. Ships that once struggled

now entered with greater reliability. State commissioners, initially skeptical, took notice. The results were hard to argue with.

Timing did the rest.

When the Erie Canal opened in 1825, Buffalo was ready. Grain and lumber poured in. Warehouses rose along the waterfront. Population surged. Commerce accelerated. The long rivalry with nearby Black Rock ended decisively. Buffalo, not Black Rock, became the canal city.

Wilkeson's influence did not end at the water's edge. As mayor in 1836, he guided Buffalo through its growing pains, helping it transition from frontier town to functioning city. He understood that infrastructure creates momentum, but governance sustains it.

His life embodied Buffalo's defining trait. Resilience.

Wilkeson took a burned-out village and willed it into a city. He absorbed loss, ridicule, and exhaustion without surrender. If Joseph Ellicott gave Buffalo its skeleton, Wilkeson gave it its beating heart. A harbor that made commerce flow, opportunity gather, and a once-marginal settlement matter.

Buffalo's later industrial rise rests quietly on this early chapter. Mud up to the knees. A blind mule. And a man who believed that persistence, applied relentlessly, could outwork doubt.

It is a small story with outsized meaning. Because long before Buffalo became resilient by reputation, it was resilient by necessity. And long before success was guaranteed, Samuel Wilkeson was already pulling forward, stone by stubborn stone, building the future the city would need.

DeWitt Clinton

Statesman of Destiny

While Samuel Wilkeson wrestled with piers, sandbars, and Lake Erie's stubborn moods, DeWitt Clinton was wrestling with something just as treacherous: politics. A towering figure in New York public life, Clinton served as Mayor of New York City, U.S. Senator, Grand Master of Masons in the State of New York, and Governor. He was ambitious, imperious, often disliked, and undeniably visionary. Few men of his era inspired such devotion and such ridicule at the same time.

Clinton's great cause was the Erie Canal. From the moment it was proposed, the project attracted scorn. Critics sneered at its scale and mocked its practicality, dismissing it as "Clinton's Ditch." How, they asked, could a single state carve a 363-mile waterway through forests, swamps, and rock? Who would finance it? Why gamble public money on an unproven dream better suited, as one critic joked, to "muskrats and frogs"?

Clinton did not retreat. He argued relentlessly that the canal would bind the Atlantic seaboard to the Great Lakes, redirecting the flow of trade away from rival ports and down the Hudson River to New York City. In doing so, it would transform New York into the Empire State and enrich farmers, merchants, and manufacturers alike. Clinton lobbied legislators, cultivated allies, secured funding, and forced the project forward through sheer political will. Where others saw wilderness, he saw leverage.

For Buffalo, Clinton's canal meant everything. The fight over the western terminus, whether it would be placed at Buffalo or nearby Black Rock, was fierce and deeply personal. Clinton listened to both sides, weighing natural advantages against engineered possibilities. In the end, the combination of Wilkeson's relentless harbor improvements and Joseph Ellicott's

ambitious city plan tipped the balance. Buffalo, small and vulnerable though it was, won the prize.

When the canal opened in 1825, Clinton staged one of the great symbolic gestures in American history. He rode in the lead boat from Buffalo to Albany carrying a keg of Lake Erie water. Upon reaching New York Harbor, he poured it into the Atlantic Ocean, ceremonially uniting inland waters with the sea in what became known as the "wedding of the waters." Cannons thundered. Church bells rang. Celebrations rippled from Manhattan to the frontier.

In that moment, Buffalo's destiny was sealed. Clinton was no Buffalonian, but his vision made the city the gateway to the West. He proved that infrastructure could rewrite geography and that political courage, when paired with imagination, could alter the course of a city and a nation.

DeWitt Clinton "wedding of the waters"

1899 - 1,500 Grain scoopers gathered at St. Bridget's Church, Louisiana Street. Buffalo Express Archive.

Bishop James Quigley:

Labor, Dignity, and Moral Backbone

By the end of the nineteenth century, Buffalo had grown into an industrial powerhouse. Grain still defined its economy, but now that grain was moved by muscle. Thousands of laborers, many of them immigrants, shoveled grain by hand from ship holds to storage. It was brutal, dangerous work.

In 1899, those grain shovelers went on strike.

What made this moment remarkable was not just the strike itself, but who stood with the workers. Bishop James Quigley, the Catholic leader of Buffalo, took a public, pro-labor stance at a time when such positions were risky. He defended the dignity of laborers and argued that economic progress did not excuse exploitation.

Quigley's intervention mattered. His moral authority shifted public perception. He framed the strike not as disorder, but as justice. Not as rebellion, but as a demand for fairness. His support helped legitimize labor's voice in a city built on industry.

This was resilience of a different kind. Not physical defense or economic gamble, but moral courage. Quigley expanded Buffalo's definition of toughness to include solidarity and conscience.

A Shared Thread: Grit With Purpose

What unites Ellicott, Chapin, Wilkeson, Clinton, and Quigley is not personality or profession. It is posture.

They acted ahead of certainty. They took risks that invited ridicule. They absorbed loss without surrender. They blurred lines between roles when necessity demanded it. They believed that cities are not just built, but defended, argued for, and stood up for.

Buffalo inherited that posture.

It shows up whenever the city refuses to disappear. Whenever neighborhoods rebuild. Whenever labor demands dignity. Whenever infrastructure is reimagined. Whenever the easy answer is to leave, and people stay instead.

This is not nostalgia. It is pattern recognition.

Buffalo's resilience is not an accident. It is a founding principle.

Buffalo was born scrappy. And it has been proving that point ever since.

Grain Elevators

Monuments of Muscle and Concrete: Buffalo's Grain Elevators and the Scoopers Who Worked Them

For more than a century, Buffalo was the place where America's bread paused to catch its breath.

Grain flowed east from the prairie heartland by lake boat, stalled at the edge of Lake Erie, then surged again through the Erie Canal and rail lines toward New York City and the world beyond. At that hinge point stood Buffalo's grain elevators, colossal structures of wood, steel, and later reinforced concrete. They were not decorative. They were instruments of movement, storage, and power. And for generations, they were worked by men whose labor was as essential as it was punishing: the scoopers.

By the early twentieth century, Buffalo had the largest grain storage capacity in the nation. More than thirty massive concrete elevators lined the Buffalo River, the inner harbor, and the outer harbor. No other city in the world processed more grain. In the 1940s and 1950s alone, more than 15,000 men worked in Buffalo's flour and feed milling industries. Grain defined the waterfront, the skyline, and the city's daily rhythm.

The elevators themselves were astonishing. Cylindrical, repetitive, and monumental, they rose straight from the water like industrial cathedrals. When the architect Le Corbusier first encountered photographs of Buffalo's concrete elevators, he famously exclaimed, "The first fruits of the new age!" To him and other modernists, these structures were pure form stripped of ornament, heroic expressions of function. To others, they were ugly monsters. Either way, they were impossible to ignore.

Their origins trace back to invention born of necessity.

When the Erie Canal opened in 1825, Buffalo exploded as a transfer point. Lake boats arriving from the Midwest carried bulk grain that had to be unloaded and transferred to canal boats bound for the Hudson River. At first, the work was brutally simple. Men, largely Irish immigrants, hauled grain in barrels by hand. It was backbreaking and slow. When the schooner Osceola arrived with one of the first bulk grain shipments, about 1,600 bushels, it took a full week to unload.

That bottleneck demanded innovation.

Buffalo entrepreneur Joseph Dart and engineer Robert Dunbar supplied it. Dart, a methodical and industrious businessman who had arrived from Connecticut in 1821, recognized the scale of what was coming. As he later reflected, the grain-producing regions of the Prairie West and Buffalo's favorable position meant eastward grain movements would soon exceed "anything the boldest imagination had conceived."

In 1842, Dart built the world's first steam-powered grain elevator. Drawing on ideas developed decades earlier by Oliver Evans, who had designed a fully automated flour mill, Dart adapted the endless bucket-and-chain lifting system to bulk grain storage. The key innovation was the marine leg, a movable arm that could swing out over a ship's hold, plunge downward, and mechanically lift grain to the top of the elevator, where it could be distributed into storage bins.

The effect was revolutionary. Grain that once took days to unload could now be moved in hours. Buffalo became indispensable.

But the machine never eliminated the man.

Once the marine leg pulled as much grain as gravity and mechanics allowed, human labor took over. Men descended into the dark, dusty holds of lake freighters to shovel, sweep, and guide the remaining grain toward the leg. By the 1860s, partial mechanization arrived in the form of giant shovels suspended on ropes or chains. These were the tools of the scoopers.

The work was precise, exhausting, and dangerous. Four men stood in the corners of the hold, each gripping a rope connected to clutch mechanisms that controlled the forward and backward motion of two massive shovels. Two additional ropes hauled the shovels themselves. Other men worked by hand, pushing grain toward the moving blades, rehanging pulleys, and constantly

1972 -Edward M. Cotter battling a blaze at General Mills

adjusting as the level dropped. At the start, the shovels ran the full length of the hold. By the end, they scraped the last stubborn grain toward the marine leg.

Except for electricity replacing steam power and lighter materials replacing iron, the system barely changed for nearly a century.

Grain handling was also perilous. Grain dust is highly combustible, and elevators were notorious for fires and explosions. The Niagara Elevator alone saw multiple disasters. One fast-moving fire had all the ingredients for catastrophe, but it was stopped in time by the fire tug William S. Grattan. That vessel was later rechristened the Edward M. Cotter, which still patrols the Buffalo River today, a living link to the era when fire and grain were constant companions.

The work sustained families, but it also bred conflict. When we speak romantically about Buffalo's "good old days," when a man could walk into a plant, put in a day's work, and provide for his family, we often forget the labor strife that accompanied that stability. Grain scoopers fought for wages, hours, and safety in conditions that took a heavy toll on bodies and lungs. Unions rose. Strikes flared. The elevators were not just machines of commerce; they were arenas of class struggle.

For decades, however, the system held. Grain poured in from the Midwest. Buffalo's elevators filled, emptied, and filled again. The Erie Canal and the elevators together collapsed a 3,000-mile journey from farm to port into a 450-mile route. Buffalo was indispensable.

Then circumstances changed.

The opening of the St. Lawrence Seaway in 1959 allowed ships to bypass Buffalo entirely, sailing directly from the Great Lakes to the Atlantic. Rail and trucking logistics improved. Grain boats stopped coming. Elevators fell silent. What had once been the city's economic engine became a stranded fleet of concrete giants.

Today, these structures stand as paradoxes. They are obsolete and indispensable. Forgotten and iconic. Architectural wonders and reminders of dangerous labor. People still stand in awe of their size and geometry, or curse them as relics cluttering the waterfront.

But the truth is simpler.

Buffalo's grain elevators fed the world. The scoopers who worked them powered a global system with muscle, coordination, and grit. Together, they transformed Buffalo from a frontier outpost into a world port, and in doing so, left behind one of the most extraordinary industrial landscapes on earth.

They are our urban castles, monuments not just to grain, but to work.

1943- Scoopers inside the nearly-emptied hatch of a grain boat unloading wheat - Library of Congress

Remembering the Many Voices

Today, as kayakers glide past restored grain elevators and families trace the boardwalks of Canalside, it is easy to forget how many lives once collided along the Buffalo River. The water appears calm now, curated and inviting, but beneath it lies a dense layering of human stories. These are stories of the Haudenosaunee who named and stewarded the waters long before canals were cut, of Black laborers who hauled and loaded cargo at the city's edge, of women whose unseen work held families together, and of immigrants who reshaped Buffalo through toil and persistence. The waterfront was never a single story. It was a chorus.

1925- Commercial Slip /Central Wharf

The Canal Arrives

When the Erie Canal opened in 1825, Buffalo was transformed almost overnight. The Commercial Slip at the foot of Main Street became the western gateway to New York's grand water highway. Packet boats arrived daily, unloading passengers, goods, and expectations from Albany, New York City, and beyond. Warehouses multiplied, docks extended outward, and grain elevators soon punctuated the shoreline. What had been a modest frontier village rapidly assumed the posture of a city.

The area surrounding the slip became known as the Canal District. It was crowded, noisy, and relentlessly productive. Thousands of immigrants, many of them Irish fleeing famine

and poverty, arrived to dig, unload, and haul. Boardinghouses, saloons, and shops sprang up to meet the needs of a transient labor force. The canal brought wealth and opportunity, but it also concentrated Buffalo's most visible inequalities at the water's edge.

Black Labor and the Geography of Freedom

The canal also carved space for Black laborers and Black aspirations. Many formerly enslaved people traveled north following the canal's current, drawn by rumors of work and relative safety. In Buffalo, they dug trenches, loaded ships, cooked aboard canal boats, and worked as sailors and stewards at the terminus docks, often earning lower wages than white workers for the same labor.

Yet the canal offered more than hardship. It formed an artery of freedom. Buffalo's position at the edge of the Niagara Frontier made it a critical link in the Underground Railroad. Black families, aided by abolitionists and sympathetic sailors, used canal boats and lake vessels to reach Canada. The waterfront became both workplace and waypoint.

Black residents established businesses and institutions that anchored community life. Michigan Street emerged as a center of Black civic and religious life, anchored by the Michigan Street Baptist Church, founded in 1831. These institutions fostered education, mutual aid, and early civil rights activism. Still, opportunity remained precarious. In the late 19th century, Black dockworkers were sometimes employed as strikebreakers during labor disputes, a practice that fueled resentment and violence. In 1891, racial tensions erupted into a riot in which Black workers were attacked, underscoring the fragility of economic gains.

Vice, Poverty, and the Infected District

By the 1830s, the canal neighborhood had earned national notoriety. Known as the Infected District, the Hooks, or simply Canal Street, it became infamous as one of the roughest waterfronts in the country, often described as "the most evil square mile in America."

Taverns, theaters, boardinghouses, and brothels crowded narrow streets. Reformers attempted to quantify the chaos. The Christian Homestead Association produced a wall-sized chart mapping every saloon and house of prostitution, marking them with red dots that revealed the district's density. Their survey counted more than 100 saloons, nearly 20 "free theater" saloons, and 75 brothels, alongside dozens of small businesses serving the same clientele.

Women of opportunity

Vice was not hidden. Saloons operated through the night. Sailors spent wages quickly. Women were not merely passive figures but active participants in the district's volatility. Arrest records show them charged with brawling, knifings, and even murder.

Poverty was equally defining. Canal Street lay within Buffalo's 19th Ward, which by the late 19th century had the city's highest concentration of tenement housing. Italian immigrants crowded into decaying structures where buildings designed for a few hundred

residents sometimes housed more than a thousand. Investigators reported water closets too filthy for use and families sleeping six to a room. Cholera and other diseases spread easily, reinforcing the district's grim name.

Women at the Water's Edge

Women's labor shaped the canal world even when it went unrecorded. They ran boardinghouses for immigrant workers, washed clothes, cooked meals, and tended injuries. In taverns along the Buffalo River, women brewed beer, kept accounts, and managed businesses while men labored on towpaths and docks. Some women even captained canal boats themselves, navigating locks and managing crews with authority that defied convention.

Closer to the river, Indigenous and immigrant women kept households in flood-prone, unsanitary conditions. They drew water, stretched scarce food, raised children, and navigated constant instability. Their lives reveal the canal not simply as an engineering triumph, but as a human landscape shaped by endurance.

Innovation on the Waterfront

The Erie Canal was not merely a trench of water; it was a laboratory of innovation. At Buffalo's harbor, engineers built breakwaters to tame Lake Erie's waves, dredged the river's mouth to accommodate larger vessels, and devised new systems for moving grain efficiently.

In the 1840s, Joseph Dart's steam-powered grain elevator revolutionized shipping. Grain that once took days to move by hand could now be transferred in hours. Buffalo became one of the busiest ports in North America, its waterfront lined with elevators that rose like industrial cathedrals.

A City Transformed and Erased

Within a generation, Buffalo was nearly unrecognizable. Canal boats carried flour, lumber, salt, and whiskey into the city; railroads soon added another layer of connectivity. The Buffalo River, once a quiet fishery for the Seneca, became an industrial corridor lined with foundries, tanneries, and elevators.

For reformers, the canal district's reputation became intolerable. Canal Street was renamed Dante Place, as if poetry might cleanse its past. Police raids came and went. Eventually, city leaders chose erasure. The Hamburg Canal was filled in. The Commercial Slip was buried beneath rubble. Buildings rose over the vanished waterway. By the early 20th century, Buffalo's original waterfront geography had been literally paved over.

Endurance Remembered

For the Haudenosaunee, the river's transformation reflected broken promises but enduring stewardship. For Black residents, it marked both opportunity and peril, labor and liberation. For women, it was a site of invisible work that sustained families. For immigrants, it was an entry point into industrial America.

Buffalo's waterfront has cycled through prosperity, vice, decline, and rebirth. Canalside now ties these threads together. What was once dismissed as the city's worst slum has become its most vibrant public square. Yet beneath the polished surface remains a layered past, waiting to be remembered, honored, and understood.

A City That Chose a Side

Buffalo and the Abolitionist Movement

Long before cannons sounded at Fort Sumter, Buffalo had already taken a stand. In the antebellum years, the city became one of the most active and consequential hubs of the abolitionist movement in the United States. Geography helped. Conviction did the rest.

Buffalo's proximity to Canada made it a crucial terminus of the Underground Railroad. Across the Niagara River lay freedom protected by British law. But Buffalo was never merely a place people passed through. It was a city where ideas were forged, strategies debated, and courage practiced daily. The fight against slavery here was not quiet or incidental. It was public, organized, and unapologetic.

The city hosted some of the most significant anti-slavery gatherings of the era. In 1843, Buffalo welcomed the National Convention of Colored Citizens, a landmark meeting that brought Black leaders together to confront slavery, disenfranchisement, and racial injustice on a national stage. Five years later, in 1848, Buffalo again found itself at the center of history when it hosted the Free Soil Party convention. An estimated 40,000 people descended on the city, rallying around the powerful slogan "Free Soil, Free Speech, Free Labor, and Free Men." The convention transformed abolition from a moral argument into a political force, helping to realign national debates and laying groundwork for future anti-slavery coalitions.

Buffalo's abolitionist energy was sustained by local action. Residents organized meetings, circulated pamphlets, raised funds, and sheltered freedom seekers. Vigilance was not a metaphor here. It was literal. After the passage of the Fugitive Slave Act of 1850, which required citizens to assist in the capture of escaped enslaved people, Buffalo's abolitionists responded with resolve. Vigilance committees formed to protect freedom seekers and resist enforcement of the law. The statute intended to strengthen slavery instead radicalized opposition to it.

At the heart of these efforts stood Buffalo's Black community. Though small in number, it was highly organized and deeply committed. Churches served as anchors of resistance. The Bethel AME Church, founded in 1831, became an early center for abolitionist organizing. Even more prominent was the Michigan Street Baptist Church, founded in 1836, which functioned as both a spiritual home and a key Underground Railroad station. Within its walls, plans were made, fugitives sheltered, and futures reclaimed. In later decades, the same institutions that fueled abolition would help seed Buffalo's early Civil Rights Movement, extending their moral reach across generations.

National figures recognized Buffalo's importance. Frederick Douglass spoke in the city repeatedly, including a major address in 1843 that helped shape abolitionist strategy and resolve. Douglass understood that Buffalo was not peripheral to the movement. It was central. From here, ideas crossed borders as surely as people crossed rivers.

What set Buffalo apart was the breadth of its commitment. The city's role extended far beyond serving as a final crossing point to Canada. Buffalo was a hotbed of intellectual, religious, and political activism against slavery. It hosted debates, conventions, sermons, and protests that pushed abolition into public consciousness and electoral politics.

In a nation divided by law and conscience, Buffalo chose conscience. It leveraged its location, its institutions, and its people to confront slavery head-on. The city's abolitionist legacy is not just a chapter in moral history. It is a reminder that progress is built where conviction meets action, and in Buffalo, that meeting place was unmistakable.

Opposite: Michigan Street Church

Forged for the Union:

Buffalo and the Crucible of the Civil War

When the Civil War erupted in 1861, Buffalo was no longer a raw frontier settlement feeling its way into relevance. It was a city hardened by water, weather, and work. Grain dust floated in the air. Ship whistles cut through the day. Rail lines, canals, and docks stitched Buffalo to the interior of a young nation. When President Abraham Lincoln issued his call for troops, Buffalo responded not hesitantly, but instinctively, as a city accustomed to moving men and material toward purpose.

Over the course of the war, Buffalo contributed more than 20,000 men to the Union cause, an extraordinary number for a city of its size. The cost was heavy. Buffalo-area soldiers suffered 4,704 casualties, a statistic that represents not abstraction but absence: empty seats at dinner tables, silent factory benches, names etched into stone and memory.

The city's response in 1861 was immediate. Drilling grounds filled almost overnight. Uniforms were sewn, muskets issued, and crowds gathered along streets and docks to watch sons and brothers march south. Among the first units to leave the region was the 21st New York Volunteers, which mobilized rapidly following Lincoln's appeal. The war's outcome was still unimaginable, but the obligation to preserve the Union was not.

Buffalo's importance extended far beyond manpower. As one of the most significant Great Lakes ports in the nation, the city became a vital industrial and logistics hub for the Union war effort. Grain from the Midwest flowed east through Buffalo, feeding both armies and civilians. Warehouses, mills, and shipyards operated at full tilt. Railroads and lake vessels carried food, uniforms, weapons, and equipment toward the front. In a war defined as much by supply as by strategy, Buffalo functioned as a hinge city, translating agricultural abundance into military endurance.

Yet the war was not fought by systems alone. It was fought by men. Few stories capture Buffalo's Civil War experience more vividly than that of Captain Michael Wiedrich and Battery I of the First New York Light Artillery.

Born in Alsace, a contested region between France and Germany, Wiedrich immigrated to the United States before the war and settled in Buffalo. He worked as a shipping clerk for Pratt & Letchworth, a job well suited to the city's commercial rhythm. When rebellion erupted, he traded ledgers for cannon.

Initially enlisting in the 65th Regiment of the New York State Militia, Wiedrich quickly proved himself capable and resolute. In 1861, he received permission from the War Department to raise his own artillery battery. Organized into approximately 140 men, most of them German immigrants from Buffalo, Battery I embodied the city's immigrant backbone. These were men who had fled European unrest only to find themselves defending a republic still defining itself.

On October 25, 1861, the battery prepared to depart. As Wiedrich's men marched through Buffalo, they sang three songs in their native

Above: Soldiers and Sailors monument, Lafayette Square. Opposite: Wiedrich Battery I of the First New York Light Artillery.

German to bid the city farewell. It was a moment thick with emotion, pride braided tightly with uncertainty. They were Buffalonians now, but they carried old languages and old loyalties with them, demonstrating that the Union cause was strengthened, not diluted, by its diversity.

At Gettysburg, Wiedrich's battery etched its name into history. Positioned on Cemetery Hill, his guns endured relentless Confederate assaults. Ammunition ran low. Horses were shot down. Infantry support wavered. Still, the battery held. Their disciplined fire helped blunt repeated attacks and played a direct role in the Union's ability to retain the high ground. It was one of those moments when a single unit's resolve helped shape the outcome of a battle, and with it, the trajectory of the war.

Buffalo's German community was not alone in its service. The city's Irish population, which comprised roughly a quarter of Buffalo's residents by 1850, also answered the call in large numbers. Irish-Americans from Buffalo served prominently throughout the Union Army, driven by loyalty to their adopted home and a belief that military service could secure their place within American society.

One of the most notable formations was the "Buffalo Irish Regiment," recruited in 1862 by Colonel John McMahon and later consolidated into the 164th New York State Volunteers, part of Corcoran's Legion. Other Buffalonians served in the 155th New York Volunteers, a regiment that endured some of the war's harshest fighting, including Cold Harbor and the Siege of Petersburg, before marching through the Appomattox Campaign toward the war's end.

At home, Buffalo bore the strain of prolonged conflict. Industry surged, but so did anxiety. News from the front arrived unevenly and often incomplete. Newspapers carried casualty lists scanned with dread. Yet the city did not falter. Endurance was already woven into Buffalo's identity. The war merely sharpened it.

By 1865, when the guns finally fell silent, Buffalo had been transformed. The city emerged forged not only by commerce and canals, but by sacrifice. Its soldiers had fought on distant fields, but their service was rooted in a local ethic: show up, do the work, hold the line.

Buffalo's contribution to the Civil War was not symbolic. It was structural. The city fed the Union, armed it, moved it, and manned it. From the docks of Lake Erie to the artillery lines at Gettysburg, Buffalo proved that victory is built slowly, day by day, by cities willing to give what they have and people willing to give what they are.In that sense, Buffalo did what it has always done best. It kept things moving. It carried the weight. And when history demanded it, it stood fast.

Beer and Breweries in Buffalo

Grain, Malt, and the Long Pour

Beer has flowed through Buffalo almost as long as people have, and for a simple reason: this city was built on grain. From the nineteenth century onward, Buffalo sat at the hinge point of North American agriculture, where Midwestern wheat and barley met eastern markets. Grain elevators rose along the waterfront not as symbols, but as necessities. Brewing followed naturally. Where grain accumulates, malt and beer soon do too.

The first breweries arrived with European immigrants, particularly Germans, Irish, and later Poles, who brought both technical knowledge and cultural expectation. Beer was familiar, affordable, and often safer than municipal water. By the mid-to-late 1800s, Buffalo supported dozens of breweries, many clustered near canals, rail lines, and grain handling facilities. Proximity mattered. Maltsters converted local barley into malt close to the elevators, reducing transport costs and ensuring freshness. Buffalo's beer economy was tightly integrated with its agricultural and industrial systems.

Local grain shaped local taste. Early Buffalo beers leaned toward lagers that emphasized balance and drinkability rather than extremes. These were beers meant for after work, for long conversations in saloons that doubled as hiring halls and community centers. Brewing was labor-intensive, and breweries employed hundreds, from coopers and bottlers to drivers and cellar workers. Beer supported families and neighborhoods as much as it supported conviviality.

Among the most prominent operations was Iroquois Brewing Company, founded in the 1880s and eventually one of the city's largest producers. Iroquois beer became synonymous with Buffalo itself, poured in taverns across the city and shipped regionally. Other breweries such as Becker, Schreiber, and Broadway served specific districts, often reflecting the ethnic makeup of their surroundings. Many sourced grain and malt through Buffalo's vast handling infrastructure, tying the taste of beer directly to the movement of crops through the harbor.

This ecosystem was fragile. Prohibition, enacted in 1920, shattered it almost overnight. Brewing halted. Malt houses closed. Grain still moved through Buffalo, but one of its most visible value-added uses disappeared. Some breweries attempted to survive by producing near-beer, soft drinks, ice, or yeast, but most never reopened. When Prohibition ended in 1933, the industry that returned was different. Consolidation favored national brands with distribution muscle, and local maltsters struggled to compete with centralized suppliers. Buffalo's brewing heritage faded into memory, even as the grain elevators still towered overhead.

By the mid-twentieth century, beer remained central to social life, but it increasingly arrived by truck from elsewhere. Industrial decline compounded the loss. As shipping patterns changed and elevators fell silent, the direct relationship between local grain, malt, and beer weakened. Brewing seemed destined to become a historical footnote, another casualty of scale and standardization.

The revival began quietly around the turn of the twenty-first century, part of a broader craft beer movement that prized locality, flavor, and story. In Buffalo, that movement found unusually fertile ground. The city still had water, space, and memory. It also had grain history embedded in its skyline. New brewers looked not only to hops and yeast, but back to barley and malt.

Flying Bison Brewing Company, founded in 2000, became a standard-bearer for this revival. Its beers referenced local identity without nostalgia, reconnecting modern brewing to Buffalo's working past. Importantly, Flying Bison and its peers helped normalize the idea that beer could once again be made here, not just consumed here.

Others followed, often deliberately tying themselves to the city's grain story. Big Ditch Brewing Company, located near Canalside, explicitly invoked the Erie Canal and the grain trade that built Buffalo. Brewing beneath the shadow of elevators, Big Ditch turned history into lived experience, serving beer where grain once passed in unimaginable quantities. The name itself is a nod to the canal era, when moving grain was the city's reason for being.

Modern Buffalo breweries increasingly engage with local and regional agriculture. While global supply chains still dominate malting, many brewers experiment with New York State barley, specialty malts, and collaborations that shorten the distance between field and glass. This reconnects beer to landscape, reminding drinkers that flavor begins long before fermentation.

What distinguishes Buffalo's beer story is continuity beneath change. The city's brewing has always depended on grain and movement, whether via canal, rail, or truck. The form shifted. The impulse did not. Even as styles evolve and tastes diversify, the foundational relationship between local grain routes and local beer culture remains legible.

Buffalo's breweries today operate in dialogue with history rather than in its shadow.

They acknowledge the grain elevators not as ruins, but as reminders of possibility. Beer here has always been about more than alcohol. It has been about work at the end of a shift, warmth in winter, and shared tables in a city that learned early how to gather.

Buffalo's beer story continues its long pour. The ingredients are familiar. The context changes. And as long as grain moves through this landscape, beer will find a way to follow.

The Railroads of Buffalo

Steel Tracks, Moving Grain, and a City in Motion

If the Erie Canal made Buffalo possible, the railroad made it powerful. By the mid-nineteenth century, rail lines stitched Buffalo into the national economy with a speed and scale canals alone could not provide. The city became not just a transfer point, but a logistical machine, where grain, coal, passengers, and manufactured goods changed direction, ownership, and destiny. Buffalo did not simply receive railroads. It was reshaped by them.

Rail arrived early. By the 1840s and 1850s, lines radiated from Buffalo in every direction, linking the city to Albany, Chicago, Pittsburgh, Toronto, and beyond. This convergence turned Buffalo into one of the most important rail hubs in North America. Goods arriving by lake were transferred to railcars; freight coming east by rail moved onward by water. The friction of transfer, so often a liability elsewhere, became Buffalo's advantage. Every delay meant jobs, warehouses, and investment.

Multiple railroads competed and cooperated here. The New York Central Railroad made Buffalo a critical eastern gateway, while the Erie Railroad tied the city to southern tier markets and the Midwest. Canadian connections added an international dimension, reinforcing Buffalo's role as a border city long before globalization became a buzzword.

Railroads accelerated industrial growth. Steel, automobiles, machinery, and consumer goods all relied on rail access. Vast switching yards sprawled across the East Side and near the waterfront, their tracks multiplying like veins. Roundhouses, depots, and repair shops employed thousands. For many working-class families, especially immigrants, railroad jobs offered steady wages and a path into the middle class. Conductors, brakemen, machinists, clerks, and porters formed their own communities, governed by schedules and seniority rather than seasons.

Passenger rail was just as transformative. Buffalo became a stopping point for travelers moving between East and Midwest, a place to change trains, eat, and sometimes stay. Grand stations rose to match that importance. The most famous was Buffalo Central Terminal, which opened in 1929. Art Deco in style and monumental in scale, the terminal symbolized peak confidence. Its soaring concourse and clock tower announced that Buffalo expected traffic to keep flowing forever.

For a brief moment, it did. Tens of thousands of passengers passed through Central Terminal daily. Trains arrived and departed around the clock. The terminal was a city within a city, complete with restaurants, shops, and offices. It was both gateway and stage set, projecting modernity and momentum.

Freight rail, however, remained the true backbone. Grain elevators relied on rail spurs to move crops efficiently. Coal fed power plants and factories. Finished goods rolled out in boxcars bearing Buffalo's name to distant markets. Railroads integrated seamlessly with the canal and lake system, making Buffalo one of the most multimodal transport hubs in the world.

That dominance carried seeds of vulnerability. As trucking expanded after World War II and highways captured long-distance freight, rail traffic declined. Passenger rail suffered even more. Automobiles and commercial aviation siphoned riders away. By the 1950s and 1960s, once-crowded stations emptied. Central

Terminal, designed for abundance, became an expensive liability.

Railroad consolidation and restructuring accelerated the decline. Yards closed. Jobs vanished. Entire neighborhoods that had grown around rail infrastructure were left exposed. In 1979, passenger service moved downtown, and Central Terminal shut its doors. The building's abandonment became a powerful symbol of Buffalo's broader economic contraction.

Yet the railroad never truly left. Freight lines still thread through the city, quieter but essential. Grain still moves. Chemicals, automobiles, and raw materials still pass through Buffalo's rail corridors. The difference is visibility. What once defined daily life now operates mostly in the background.

In recent years, Buffalo has begun to reassess its rail legacy with clearer eyes. Preservation efforts at Central Terminal aim to stabilize and reimagine the structure not as a relic, but as an asset. Rail corridors are reconsidered as potential transit routes, trails, or development spines. The question is no longer whether rail mattered, but how its imprint can be reused intelligently.

The history of railroads in Buffalo is a study in scale and adaptation. Tracks brought opportunity, labor, and wealth. They also concentrated risk when economic patterns shifted. But even in decline, rail shaped the city's physical and social landscape too deeply to erase.

Buffalo learned to live by schedules, whistles, and timetables. Neighborhoods rose and fell with yard activity. Generations measured time by departures and arrivals. Today, when freight trains still rumble through the city at night, they carry echoes of that era.

The railroad story is not over. It has simply slowed, changed lanes, and waited. Like Buffalo itself, it remains embedded, durable, and ready, should the moment come, to move again.

The Buffalo Fire Department

Flames, Brotherhood, and a City Built to Burn

The history of the Buffalo Fire Department is written in ash and resolve. From its earliest days, Buffalo was a city uniquely vulnerable to fire. Wood-framed buildings, dense neighborhoods, grain dust, lumber yards, and fierce lake winds created conditions where a single spark could level entire blocks. Firefighting here was never ceremonial. It was existential.

In Buffalo's earliest years, fire protection relied on volunteer companies, bucket brigades, and hand-drawn engines. These crews were often neighborhood-based, fiercely proud, and intensely competitive. While camaraderie ran deep, coordination was inconsistent, and response times varied. As Buffalo exploded in population during the mid-nineteenth century, fueled by the Erie Canal and industrial growth, the limitations of volunteer fire protection became impossible to ignore.

The professional Buffalo Fire Department was established in 1863, marking a turning point. Paid firefighters replaced volunteers, stations were standardized, and discipline replaced rivalry. The change reflected a growing understanding that fire protection was essential urban infrastructure, not a civic hobby. Firefighters became municipal employees tasked with safeguarding a city whose wealth was increasingly stacked in combustible forms.

The challenges were immense. Buffalo's grain elevators posed unprecedented risks. Fine grain dust, suspended in air, could ignite explosively. Lumber docks burned hot and fast. Factories operated around the clock. Firefighters confronted blazes that were as much industrial disasters as structural fires. Innovations in equipment and tactics often followed catastrophe, with lessons learned under extreme conditions.

The late nineteenth and early twentieth centuries were formative. Horse-drawn steam engines gave way to motorized apparatus. Alarm

Amoskeag Horseless Fire Engine - 1897

The first hand-drawn pumper was acquired in 1824, effectively creating Engine No. 1

systems improved. Training became more formal. Firehouses doubled as community anchors, places where firefighters lived, trained, and forged lifelong bonds. Many firefighters were drawn from Irish, German, Polish, and Italian working-class neighborhoods, continuing a tradition where public service offered stability, pride, and identity.

Buffalo's firefighters earned national respect for their work in extreme conditions. Winter added another layer of difficulty. Frozen hydrants, icy ladders, and bitter winds turned every response into a test of endurance. Fire did not pause for weather, and neither did the department.

Mid-century shifts brought new challenges. Urban renewal altered street grids and building stock. High-rise construction introduced vertical firefighting, requiring new equipment and strategies. At the same time, population loss and industrial decline reduced resources even as aging infrastructure increased risk. Fires in abandoned buildings became common, dangerous, and unpredictable.

Despite these pressures, the Buffalo Fire Department remained deeply embedded in civic life. Firefighters were not distant figures. They were neighbors, relatives, and familiar faces. Open houses, parades, and station traditions reinforced public trust. The department's culture emphasized service, sacrifice, and solidarity, values passed from one generation to the next.

Tragedy has shaped the department's memory. Line-of-duty deaths left lasting marks, reminding the city of the risks firefighters accept routinely. Each loss reinforced a collective understanding that firefighting is not just a job, but a calling with real cost.

Today, the Buffalo Fire Department operates in a city balancing revival with vulnerability. New development brings modern materials and codes, while older neighborhoods still carry legacy risks. Climate change introduces more extreme weather, adding complexity to response. Yet the department continues to adapt, blending tradition with innovation.

The history of the Buffalo Fire Department mirrors Buffalo itself: shaped by industry, tested by adversity, and sustained by community. When fires break out, the city still relies on the same essential promise made in 1863: that someone will come, no matter the conditions, to stand between flame and home.

The Buffalo Police Department

Order, Authority, and a City in Motion

The history of the Buffalo Police Department is inseparable from the history of the city it serves. Founded in the mid-nineteenth century as Buffalo grew from canal town to industrial powerhouse, the department evolved alongside waves of immigration, labor unrest, and urban expansion. Policing here was never abstract. It was shaped by docks, factories, neighborhoods, and the constant movement of people and goods.

Before formal organization, law enforcement in Buffalo relied on constables, night watchmen, and ad hoc patrols. As population surged in the 1840s and 1850s, particularly with Irish and German immigration, those systems proved inadequate. The modern Buffalo Police Department emerged to impose order in a dense, rapidly changing city where crime, fire, and public disorder were daily concerns. Early officers walked beats on foot, enforcing curfews, breaking up fights, and responding to emergencies with limited resources and broad discretion.

1860s Buffalo Police Uniform

By the late nineteenth century, the department professionalized. Uniforms standardized. Ranks formalized. Telegraphs and patrol wagons improved response times. Policing intersected directly with labor and politics. Officers were called to manage strikes, quell unrest, and maintain access to docks and rail yards during periods of intense conflict. These moments forged a complicated relationship between police and working-class neighborhoods, particularly immigrant communities who viewed authority with skepticism shaped by Old World experience.

The early twentieth century brought further change. Automobiles replaced foot patrols. Radios transformed communication. The department expanded specialized units to address traffic, vice, and organized crime. Prohibition intensified enforcement pressures, placing officers at the center of conflicts over alcohol that blurred the line between law and daily life in a city where taverns were social anchors.

Mid-century Buffalo saw policing shaped by suburbanization and demographic shifts. As residents moved outward, the city's tax base shrank, concentrating poverty and social challenges in the urban core. The police department increasingly confronted issues of race, inequality, and mistrust, particularly as the Civil Rights era exposed systemic disparities nationwide. These tensions were not unique to Buffalo, but they played out locally in neighborhoods already burdened by disinvestment and segregation.

In recent decades, the Buffalo Police Department has wrestled with evolving expectations. Community policing initiatives sought to rebuild trust through presence and engagement rather than force alone. Technological advances introduced data-driven strategies, body cameras, and new accountability measures. At the same time, high-profile incidents and public protests forced difficult conversations about use of force, transparency, and the role of police in modern civic life.

Tragedy has also shaped the department's identity. Officers have died in the line of duty. Others have become symbols in broader debates about public safety and justice. Each moment added layers to a history already marked by complexity rather than clarity.

Today, the Buffalo Police Department operates in a city that continues to redefine itself. Downtown revival, neighborhood reinvestment, and demographic change all influence how policing is perceived and practiced. The department's challenge remains what it has always been: balancing enforcement with legitimacy, authority with restraint, and safety with trust.

The history of the Buffalo Police is not a simple progression from past to present. It is a record of adaptation under pressure, reflecting Buffalo's own struggles and aspirations. Like the city, the department carries both legacy and burden, shaped by the streets it patrols and the people who call those streets home.

Fire on the Waterfront

The Rise and Fall of Steelmaking in Buffalo

For much of the twentieth century, steel was not just an industry in Buffalo. It was an atmosphere. It glowed at night, rattled windows by day, and coated neighborhoods in a fine grit that settled into brick, lungs, and memory. Steel shaped Buffalo's skyline, its labor culture, and its sense of purpose. It promised permanence. And then, almost unthinkably, it vanished.

Buffalo's rise as a steelmaking center was no accident. Geography had been recruiting for the industry long before the first blast furnace was lit. Iron ore from Minnesota's Mesabi Range moved east across the Great Lakes. Coal arrived from Pennsylvania and Appalachia. Limestone flowed in from Ontario. Buffalo sat at the hinge point, where lake met rail, canal met river. Raw materials converged here naturally, as if the city itself had been designed for fire and metal.

By the early 1900s, steelmaking had begun to dominate the southern edge of the city and the adjacent towns of Lackawanna and Tonawanda. The waterfront transformed into an industrial rampart. Towers rose. Furnaces flared. Rail spurs multiplied like roots seeking fuel. What had once been marshland and working docks became one of the most concentrated steel corridors in the nation.

The crown jewel was Bethlehem Steel's Lackawanna plant, which opened in 1903 just south of Buffalo's city line. At its peak, the complex stretched nearly four miles along the lake and employed more than 20,000 workers. It was, at the time, one of the largest steel plants in the world. The scale defied easy description. Ore boats docked like floating buildings. Blast furnaces roared continuously, some operating for decades without ever being shut down. The plant produced steel plate, rails, wire, and structural components that built bridges, ships, skyscrapers, and war machines.

Steel jobs were hard, dangerous, and coveted. They paid well. They offered stability. They came with a sense of pride that was hard to exaggerate. Men worked twelve-hour shifts in heat that could peel paint. Sparks burned holes through clothing. The work aged bodies quickly, but it built families, neighborhoods, and entire lives. Steelworkers bought homes, filled parish schools, sponsored bowling teams, and anchored a dense web of ethnic and labor identity on Buffalo's South Buffalo and Lackawanna streets.

World War I and World War II supercharged the industry. Buffalo's steel fed American victory abroad and economic confidence at home. During World War II, production surged as steel flowed into tanks, ships, weapons, and infrastructure. The waterfront never slept. Shift whistles replaced church bells as the city's metronome. Buffalo did not merely support the Arsenal of Democracy. It forged it.

By the postwar years, steel seemed invincible. Demand was global. America dominated production. Buffalo's mills stood at the center of a national system that appeared unassailable. Entire communities were organized around shift changes and mill gates. Sons followed fathers into the plants. Retirement was expected, not hoped for. The furnaces had always been there. Why would they ever go out?

The answer arrived slowly at first, then all at once.

By the late 1950s and early 1960s, cracks began to show. Foreign competition intensified as Europe and Japan rebuilt with newer, more efficient steel plants. Buffalo's mills, once state-of-the-art, were aging. Retrofitting them required massive capital investment, and corporate leadership increasingly hesitated. The industry that had once prided itself on permanence had grown cautious, even complacent.

At the same time, technological shifts reduced the need for labor. Continuous casting, automation, and changes in manufacturing meant fewer workers could produce more steel elsewhere. Global shipping costs dropped. Steel no longer had to be made close to where it was used. Buffalo's geographic advantage narrowed.

Labor relations, once a source of strength, became strained. Unions fought fiercely to protect wages, benefits, and jobs they had earned through decades of dangerous work. Management pushed back, citing costs and competitiveness. Neither side was wrong. Both were trapped in a system that was changing faster than either wanted to admit.

Then came the 1970s.

A combination of recession, inflation, foreign imports, and corporate restructuring hit the American steel industry like a hammer. Plants closed across the Rust Belt. In Buffalo, layoffs mounted. Temporary shutdowns became permanent. Furnaces that had burned continuously for generations were idled, then dismantled. The emotional shock was profound. This was not just job loss. It was identity loss.

Bethlehem Steel began scaling back operations in Lackawanna in the late 1970s. Employment plummeted. Entire departments vanished. By the early 1980s, the writing was unmistakable. In 1983, Bethlehem announced the closure of most operations at the Lackawanna plant. Thousands of workers were laid off. Families who had done everything "right" found themselves stranded. Skills honed over decades suddenly had nowhere to go.

The ripple effects tore through the region. Small businesses closed. Property values collapsed. Municipal tax bases shrank. Young people left in waves. Buffalo's population, which had peaked in the mid-twentieth century, fell sharply. Steel's decline accelerated a broader economic unraveling that would define the city's national reputation for decades.

The physical aftermath was just as stark. Miles of abandoned industrial land stretched along the lake, contaminated and silent. Rusting structures loomed over empty lots. What had once been a symbol of power became a visual shorthand for loss. The term "Rust Belt" stuck, and Buffalo wore it heavily. Yet even in collapse, steel left something durable behind.

The culture of work it created did not disappear. It adapted. Former steelworkers retrained, started small businesses, or carried their mechanical skills into other industries. The ethic of showing up, doing dangerous work well, and watching out for one another persisted. It reappeared in construction, transportation, healthcare, and advanced manufacturing. The steel may have gone cold, but the muscle memory remained.

In recent years, Buffalo has begun to reclaim its waterfront, not by erasing its steel past, but by reinterpreting it. The former Bethlehem Steel site has become the focus of redevelopment, including renewable energy projects and public access. Grain elevators, once feeding furnaces and ships, now stand as monuments, repurposed for culture, tourism, and reflection. The city no longer turns its back on its industrial scars. It frames them.

The rise and fall of steelmaking in Buffalo is not a simple morality tale about bad decisions or inevitable decline. It is a story about scale, timing, and change. Steel built Buffalo into a world-class industrial city. Steel sustained it through war and prosperity. And steel, when it retreated, forced Buffalo to confront who it was without it.

That reckoning has been long and painful. But it has also revealed something essential. Buffalo was never just a steel town. It was a town of builders. Steel was the tool. The people were the constant.

The furnaces may be silent now, but the city they forged is still standing.

Pan-American Exposition of 1901

The City of Light and Its Shadows

In 1901, Buffalo staged a spectacle meant to announce the twentieth century with confidence and electricity. The Pan-American Exposition was a technological triumph, a civic coming-out party, and a declaration that Buffalo belonged among the great cities of the modern world. Yet beneath the glow of 100,000 electric bulbs lay a darker current. The fair celebrated progress while quietly reinforcing racial hierarchies that mirrored the inequalities of the age. Buffalo's City of Light also cast long shadows.

Power, Optimism, and Display

Built on 350 acres near Delaware Park, the exposition dazzled visitors with color, symmetry, and innovation. Architects abandoned the white neoclassical palette of earlier fairs in favor of warm yellows, reds, and blues that came alive under electric illumination. At the center rose the Electric Tower, a beacon of modernity powered by hydroelectric energy from Niagara Falls. At night, the grounds glowed steadily, convincing millions that technology could master nature itself.

The exposition framed industry as benevolent and orderly. Buffalo's identity as a hub of grain, steel, rail, and shipping was polished into a narrative of inevitable progress. More than eight million visitors attended between May and November, sampling foods, watching performances, and touring exhibits from across the Western Hemisphere. The message was clear: the future was bright, American-led, and electrified.

The Pan-American Idea and Its Limits

The fair's theme emphasized unity and commerce among the nations of the Americas. In theory, it

Pan-Am Parade

promoted hemispheric cooperation. In practice, it reflected the racial assumptions and imperial confidence of the era. While European and North American achievements were showcased as symbols of advancement, nonwhite cultures were often presented as curiosities, frozen in time, or placed on a supposed evolutionary ladder beneath Western civilization.

This was not unique to Buffalo. World's fairs of the late nineteenth and early twentieth centuries routinely used ethnographic displays and "living exhibits" to reinforce ideas of racial superiority. The Pan-American Exposition followed that pattern. On the Midway, visitors encountered attractions that blurred entertainment and anthropology, presenting Indigenous peoples, Afro-Caribbean communities, and others through a colonial lens that emphasized difference over dignity.

These displays were framed as educational, but they traded in stereotypes. They suggested that progress flowed in one direction and that some peoples existed primarily as contrasts to modernity. The fair celebrated electricity and empire in the same breath, revealing how technological optimism could coexist comfortably with racial exclusion.

Black Buffalo at the Margins

For Buffalo's Black residents, the exposition was a complicated moment. The city had a strong abolitionist legacy and a history of Black civic leadership. Yet at the fair, African Americans were largely absent from positions of authority and representation. Their contributions to American life, industry, and culture were not given equal platform. When Black people appeared in the exposition's narrative, it was often through the distorted lens of the Midway rather than as full participants in modern progress.

This exclusion echoed broader national realities. The exposition took place during the height of Jim Crow segregation, only five years after the Supreme Court's Plessy v. Ferguson decision sanctioned "separate but equal." While Buffalo prided itself on modernity, it did not fundamentally challenge the racial order of its time. Progress was selective.

Triumph Interrupted - The Temple of Music

Among the exposition's most elegant structures was the Temple of Music, a domed concert hall designed for performances and public addresses. It was here, on September 6, 1901, that the exposition's story took a tragic turn that would forever bind Buffalo to a moment of national shock.

President William McKinley, a popular and recently re-elected leader, visited the exposition as part of a goodwill tour. The fair represented everything his administration championed: growth, stability, and American confidence. After delivering a speech earlier in the day, McKinley entered the Temple of Music to greet the public in a receiving line.

Among those waiting was Leon Czolgosz, an anarchist who concealed a revolver beneath a handkerchief. When his turn came, he fired two shots at close range. McKinley was mortally wounded.

At first, there was hope. Doctors believed the president might recover. Buffalo held its breath. The nation waited. But infection set in, and on September 14, McKinley died in a Buffalo home where he had been taken to recover.

The shock was profound. The exposition closed temporarily. Flags drooped. The city that had been bathed in electric optimism found itself plunged into mourning. Vice President Theodore Roosevelt was sworn in as president in Buffalo, at the Wilcox Mansion, abruptly ushering in a new political era.

A Fair Remembered for Light and Loss

The assassination irrevocably altered the legacy of the Pan-American Exposition. What had been intended as a triumphant symbol of progress became inseparable from tragedy. For decades, the fair was remembered less for its innovations than for the moment that ended a presidency and reshaped American politics.

Yet to reduce the exposition to that single event is to miss its deeper significance.

The Pan-American Exposition was a milestone in the history of electricity, urban planning, and public spectacle. It demonstrated how power could be integrated into daily life, not just factories. It influenced future fairs and cities alike, accelerating the adoption of electric lighting across the country. It showcased Buffalo at its most confident, when the city believed that growth, technology, and civic ambition pointed in the same direction.

The fair also revealed the fragility beneath that confidence. The same openness that welcomed millions also allowed violence to intrude. The same belief in progress could not prevent chaos. In this way, the exposition captured the tension of the new century itself: astonishing capability paired with unresolved risk.

Empire, Race, and the New Century

The Pan-American Exposition unfolded at a moment when the United States was asserting itself as a global power. The Spanish-American War had ended just three years earlier. American influence now extended into the Caribbean and Pacific. The fair's emphasis on the Western Hemisphere was inseparable from this imperial confidence.

Racial hierarchy underpinned that worldview. Technological progress was presented as evidence of moral and cultural superiority. The fair's design, exhibits, and omissions reinforced a story in which white, industrialized nations led history forward while others followed or stood still. Electricity lit the buildings, but ideology lit the narrative.

After the Lights Went Out

When the exposition closed, most of its buildings were dismantled. The Electric Tower disappeared. The grounds returned to parkland. What endured was memory, uneven and conflicted. For decades, the exposition was remembered primarily for McKinley's assassination and the spectacle of electric light. Its racial exclusions were rarely discussed.

Yet those omissions matter. The Pan-American Exposition reveals how Buffalo, like the nation itself, could be both forward-looking and constrained by inherited prejudice. It shows that modernity does not automatically produce justice, and that innovation can coexist with inequality.

Reckoning with the Whole Story

Today, as Buffalo revisits its history with clearer eyes, the Pan-American Exposition stands as a layered symbol. It represents ambition, ingenuity, and confidence. It also reflects the blind spots of an era that equated progress with hierarchy.

To remember the exposition honestly is not to diminish its achievements, but to understand them fully. The City of Light shone brilliantly in 1901, but its shadows tell us just as much about who was allowed to stand in that light and who was pushed to its edges.

Buffalo's challenge, then and now, is not simply to celebrate progress, but to ask who it serves.

Opposite: President McKinley addressing the crowd for what would be his last speech, September 5, 1901

A Sudden Oath in Borrowed Clothes

Theodore Roosevelt Becomes President in Buffalo

Few inaugurations in American history were as abrupt, intimate, or consequential as the one that took place in Buffalo on September 14, 1901. There were no crowds, no parade, and no Bible. Instead, there was urgency, borrowed clothing, and a quiet room where the presidency changed hands in the shadow of national grief.

Following the death of President William McKinley, Vice President Theodore Roosevelt was summoned back to Buffalo with all possible speed. Roosevelt had been hiking in the Adirondacks when word reached him that McKinley's condition had worsened. By the time he arrived in Buffalo, the president had already died in the early hours of the morning.

The transition could not wait. The Constitution required continuity, and the country was watching.

Roosevelt, only 42 years old, arrived without appropriate formal attire for such a solemn occasion. In his haste, there had been no time to prepare. To appear suitable for the office he was about to assume, Roosevelt borrowed clothing from local men: a frock coat, waistcoat, striped trousers, and shoes. The image is striking. A future giant of American political history stepping into the presidency dressed, quite literally, in someone else's clothes.

The oath of office was administered that afternoon at the home of Anselm Wilcox, a prominent Buffalo lawyer and civic figure. In the front library of the Wilcox House, Judge John R. Hazel of the U.S. District Court gathered a small group of witnesses that included cabinet members, local officials, and friends. The room was modest. The mood was restrained. Outside, Buffalo stood in mourning.

Because none was immediately available with such short notice, no Bible was used during the ceremony. Roosevelt simply raised his right hand. There was no speech. No flourish. Roosevelt just swore to "faithfully execute the office of President of the United States" and to preserve, protect, and defend the Constitution. With those words, spoken quietly in a Buffalo library, the nation entered a new political era. For his second term he placed his hand on the Washington Bible.

The symbolism of the moment is profound. Roosevelt assumed the presidency at the Pan-American Exposition's host city, just days after that celebration of modernity had been shattered by violence. The electric glow of the fair had given way to somber stillness. Yet from that stillness emerged a president who would redefine the office.

Roosevelt's inauguration marked a generational shift. He brought energy, reformist zeal, and a willingness to use federal power in ways his predecessors had avoided. Trust-busting, conservation, labor mediation, and an expanded global presence all followed. Much of what Americans now recognize as the modern presidency traces back to this unplanned moment in Buffalo.

Today, the Wilcox House stands preserved as the Theodore Roosevelt Inaugural National Historic Site. Visitors can stand in the same library where Roosevelt raised his hand, wearing borrowed clothes, and accepted responsibility rather than celebration.

It is a reminder that history does not always unfold with ceremony. Sometimes it arrives breathless, improvised, and solemn. In Buffalo, on a September afternoon in 1901, the presidency changed hands not with grandeur, but with resolve, proving that democracy's strength lies not in ritual alone, but in its ability to endure sudden moments of necessity.

Opposite: Roosevelt's inauguration took place in the library of the Wilcox House

Albright-Knox Art Gallery

Buffalo's Modern Conscience

Few institutions have shaped Buffalo's cultural identity as profoundly or as consistently as the Albright-Knox Art Gallery. Long before Buffalo was described as a "comeback city," the Albright-Knox made a quiet, contrarian decision. It would not chase safe tastes or retrospective comfort. Instead, it would collect the art of its own time. That commitment, radical when it began and still demanding today, positioned Buffalo as an unlikely yet enduring center of modern and contemporary art.

A Temple Built for Art

The story begins with architecture. The gallery's original neoclassical building, designed by E. B. Green and opened to the public in 1905, sits at the edge of Delaware Park like a civic temple. Its columns and symmetry speak the language of permanence, signaling that art was not a luxury but a public good. Conceived as part of the cultural legacy of the Pan-American Exposition era, the building reflected a city that believed progress was not only industrial or economic, but intellectual and aesthetic.

Yet from the outset, the institution resisted becoming a mausoleum for the past. While many American museums focused on Old Masters and historical collections, the Albright-Knox oriented itself toward the present. Its architecture may have evoked tradition, but its mission quietly rejected it.

1913 Photo

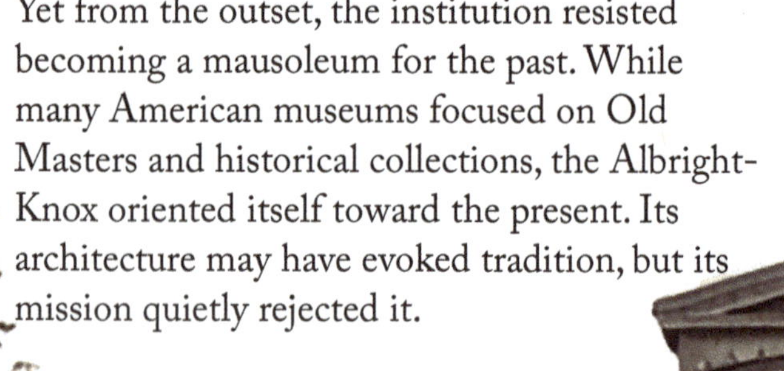

Seymour H. Knox Jr. and a Dangerous Idea

That forward-looking posture crystallized under the influence of Seymour H. Knox Jr., whose name the gallery would later adopt. Knox championed a deceptively simple but deeply risky idea: collect art by living artists. At a time when modern art was frequently dismissed as incomprehensible, vulgar, or outright fraudulent, this approach required confidence, patience, and a tolerance for controversy.

The gallery began acquiring works by artists who would later define twentieth-century art, often before their reputations were secure. These were not trophies of consensus but acts of belief. Some choices sparked backlash. Others puzzled visitors. Many paid off spectacularly. Together they established the Albright-Knox as an institution that trusted artists over trends and conviction over comfort.

Modern Art in an Industrial City

That such a collection took root in Buffalo is no accident, though it often surprises outsiders. In the early twentieth century, Buffalo was wealthy, confident, and globally connected. Industrial success had created patrons accustomed to risk, scale, and innovation. The city understood systems, infrastructure, and experimentation. The Albright-Knox reflected that mentality. It was never meant to reassure. It was meant to provoke.

For generations of Buffalonians, first encounters with abstraction, modern sculpture, or challenging contemporary work happened not in coastal capitals but on Elmwood Avenue. School trips, college assignments, and weekend visits became formative experiences. The museum did not tell visitors what to think. It taught them how to look.

The Collection as Argument

The Albright-Knox's collection functions less like a comprehensive survey and more like an argument about what matters. Strengths in postwar abstraction, pop art, minimalism, and contemporary practice reveal consistent priorities: innovation, formal rigor, and intellectual seriousness. Rather than attempting to represent everything, the museum chose depth over breadth.

That decision had consequences. In lean years, the gallery faced criticism for what it did not collect as much as for what it did. Questions of representation, accessibility, and relevance grew louder in the late twentieth and early twenty-first centuries. Instead of retreating from its identity, the institution widened its lens while holding fast to its core belief: that contemporary art is not optional to civic life, but essential.

Expansion and Reinvention

That belief ultimately shaped the gallery's most ambitious transformation. In the 2010s and early 2020s, the institution undertook a sweeping expansion that reimagined both its physical footprint and its civic role. Reopening as the AKG Art Museum marked more than a rebrand. It signaled a philosophical evolution.

New buildings and public spaces transformed the museum into a campus rather than a single monument. Exhibition space expanded dramatically, allowing more of the collection to be visible at any given time. Transparent façades, outdoor sculpture, and integrated public areas blurred the boundary between museum and park. Art spilled outward, inviting engagement rather than demanding pilgrimage.

Art as Public Infrastructure

One of the AKG's most consequential decisions was the elimination of general admission fees. In doing so, the museum reaffirmed its founding principle that art belongs to everyone. The impact was immediate and visible. Audiences diversified. Casual visits increased. The museum became part of daily life rather than a special occasion.

Outdoor installations along Elmwood Avenue and throughout the campus reinforced that idea. Sculptures became wayfinding landmarks. Art entered commutes, jogs, and afternoon strolls. The museum functioned less as a destination apart from the city and more as cultural infrastructure woven into its rhythms.

A Global Voice, a Local Anchor

Despite its international stature, the Albright-Knox has remained deeply local. Its proximity to Delaware Park, Elmwood Village, and surrounding neighborhoods ensures constant interaction. Families picnic beside installations. Children grow up seeing art not as distant or intimidating, but familiar.

At the same time, the museum places Buffalo in global conversation. Visiting artists, curators, and scholars encounter a city that understands contemporary art not as an accessory to success, but as evidence of civic seriousness.

Continuity Through Change

Across more than a century, the Albright-Knox has demonstrated rare institutional consistency. Names changed. Buildings expanded. Audiences evolved. But the underlying philosophy remained intact. Collect the art of now. Trust artists early. Treat the public as capable.

That consistency has not been easy. It required weathering criticism, financial pressure, and cultural shifts. What it produced, however, is something enduring: a museum that reflects Buffalo at its best. Serious without being elitist. Ambitious without being flashy. Willing to evolve without abandoning its spine.

A Measure of the City

To understand the Albright-Knox is to understand Buffalo's relationship with risk, creativity, and public life. The gallery stands as proof that a city once defined by industry chose to invest in ideas. It reminds Buffalo that reinvention is not only economic, but cultural.

In the end, the Albright-Knox does not merely display art. It models a way of thinking. It insists that the present matters, that experimentation is worth discomfort, and that a city's imagination deserves permanent shelter. For more than a century, Buffalo has carried that belief in stone, steel, canvas, and light.

Opposite: Buffalo AKG Art Museum, Jeffrey E. Gundlach Building - 2023

BUFFALO AKG ART MUSEUM
JEFFREY E. GUNDLACH
BUILDING

CJ

The Buffalo Colored Musicians Club

Where the Music Never Asked for Permission

Tucked modestly into a residential block on Michigan Avenue, the Buffalo Colored Musicians Club holds a distinction that is easy to miss and impossible to overstate. Founded in 1917, it is the oldest continuously operating African American musicians club in the United States. Long before jazz became a museum piece or a college syllabus, this building functioned as a refuge, a workshop, and a proving ground for Black musicians navigating a segregated entertainment world.

The club emerged during an era when African American musicians were routinely barred from white unions, hotels, and performance halls, even as their music fueled American popular culture. In Buffalo, as in many cities, Black musicians needed a place where they could rehearse, organize gigs, share information, and simply exist without constraint. The Colored Musicians Club provided exactly that. It was part union hall, part social club, part sanctuary. Music was the entry fee. Respect was guaranteed.

Inside its walls, generations of musicians honed their craft. Jazz, blues, swing, bebop, and later styles flowed through the room, evolving in real time. Touring legends passing through Buffalo found their way there after formal gigs ended, when the real music began. Jam sessions stretched late into the night, unrecorded but unforgettable. Stories circulate of impromptu performances by national figures who wanted to play freely, away from contracts, expectations, and color lines.

The club's influence extended far beyond sound. It offered structure in a profession defined by instability. Members shared leads, supported one another during lean times, and cultivated younger players. In a city shaped by segregation and inequality, the club functioned as an institution of self-determination. It did not wait for permission to exist or validation from outside power structures. It built its own legitimacy, one performance at a time.

As Buffalo's jazz scene waxed and waned through the decades, the Colored Musicians Club endured. When downtown clubs closed, when musical tastes shifted, when urban renewal erased Black neighborhoods nearby, the club remained. Its survival was not accidental. It reflected a deep sense of ownership among its members and the surrounding community, who understood that losing the club would mean losing a living archive.

In recent decades, renewed attention has brought wider recognition. The club has been designated a historic landmark and embraced as a cultural treasure not just for Buffalo, but for the nation. Performances today draw diverse audiences, bridging generations and backgrounds. The music remains central, but so does the history embedded in the walls.

The Colored Musicians Club reminds Buffalo that culture is not only what happens on grand stages or under bright marquees. Sometimes it happens in small rooms where the door stays open and the groove stays steady. For more than a century, this club has kept time for the city, preserving a lineage of sound, struggle, and creativity that refuses to fade.

Opposite: 1950s jam session with jazz greats Dizzy Gillespie, John Coltrane, and Miles Davis.

Hand, Heart, and Hammer

The Roycroft Movement in East Aurora

At the turn of the twentieth century, as America raced headlong into mechanization, one small village in Western New York chose a different tempo. In East Aurora, the clatter of factory belts gave way to the measured rhythm of hand tools, ink presses, and burnished copper. Here, the Roycroft movement took root, offering not nostalgia, but a principled alternative to industrial excess. It was a place where work was meant to be meaningful, objects were meant to last, and culture was meant to be made by hand.

The Roycroft story begins with Elbert Hubbard, a restless, persuasive figure who believed that ideas should be lived, not merely written. After a successful stint in soap manufacturing, Hubbard turned toward letters, philosophy, and design. Inspired by William Morris and the British Arts and Crafts movement, he envisioned a community where craftsmanship, ethics, and enterprise could coexist. He found his canvas in East Aurora, a rail-linked village close enough to Buffalo to draw visitors and far enough away to define itself on its own terms.

Founded in 1895, the Roycroft enterprise began modestly as a printing operation. Hubbard's magazine, The Philistine, was equal parts satire, social critique, and provocation. It attracted readers hungry for wit and independence in an era of conformity. Soon followed the Roycroft Press, producing books that were unapologetically tactile. Thick handmade paper. Leather bindings. Type set with care. These were volumes meant to be felt as much as read.

But Roycroft did not stop at ink and paper. It expanded into a full-fledged campus of workshops and guilds. Furniture makers crafted sturdy, rectilinear pieces that emphasized joinery over ornament. Metalworkers hammered copper into lamps and desk sets that glowed with warmth rather than polish. Leatherworkers tooled belts and book covers meant to age gracefully. Even the architecture followed the philosophy: simple forms, honest materials, and buildings that felt grown rather than imposed.

At its height, Roycroft employed hundreds of artisans. Some came for a season. Others stayed for years. Many lived on or near the campus, creating a rare synthesis of work, life, and community. The Roycroft was not a commune in the strict sense, but it functioned as a village

Above: Elbert Hubbard. Opposite: Copper Shop workers

within a village. Meals were shared. Lectures were held. Music drifted through open windows. Ideas were argued late into the night.

Hubbard himself was the movement's chief catalyst and lightning rod. He wrote incessantly, delivering aphorisms that were sharp enough to sting and broad enough to circulate widely. "Do not take life too seriously," he quipped, "you will never get out of it alive." His most famous essay, A Message to Garcia, extolled initiative and duty, becoming required reading in boardrooms and military academies alike. Critics accused Hubbard of simplifying complex ideas into slogans. Admirers countered that he understood something essential about motivation and meaning in modern life.

What made Roycroft distinct was its embrace of commerce without surrendering ideals. Unlike some Arts and Crafts experiments that rejected the marketplace entirely, Roycroft engaged it boldly. Goods were sold through catalogs and showrooms across the country. Visitors arrived by train, eager to see the campus and meet the artisans. The Roycroft Inn, with its heavy timbers and welcoming hearth, became both a destination and a manifesto in wood and stone.

This balance between idealism and pragmatism was not without tension. As demand grew, the pressure to produce more tested the limits of handcraft. Hubbard navigated these contradictions with characteristic confidence, arguing that honest work done well could scale without losing its soul. Whether that balance was fully achieved remains debated, but the attempt itself marked Roycroft as unusually American in spirit: aspirational, entrepreneurial,

Above: Roycroft Print Shop

Hand-Binding Roycroft books

and argumentative by design.

The movement also challenged prevailing social norms. Women played prominent roles as artisans, writers, and managers within the Roycroft community. Intellectual independence was encouraged. Nonconformity was celebrated. In an era of rigid social hierarchies, East Aurora became a place where ideas mattered more than pedigree and skill carried its own authority.

The First World War marked a turning point. In 1915, Elbert Hubbard and his wife, Alice Moore Hubbard, boarded the RMS Lusitania en route to Europe and perished when the ship was sunk by a German submarine. The loss was sudden and profound. Without its founder's energy and voice, Roycroft struggled to maintain momentum. The cultural climate shifted. Modernism rose. Mass production refined itself. The very forces Roycroft had resisted grew more efficient and more seductive.

By the 1930s, the movement had largely faded as a commercial enterprise. Workshops closed. Artisans dispersed. What remained was the physical campus and a philosophy that refused to vanish quietly. Buildings endured. Furniture survived in homes and museums. Ideas resurfaced whenever Americans questioned the cost of convenience and the meaning of work.

Today, East Aurora still bears the imprint of Roycroft. The campus has been preserved and revitalized, its buildings repurposed for gatherings, shops, and reflection. Visitors walk the grounds and sense that this was not merely a factory or a school, but an argument made in brick, oak, and ink. The Roycroft legacy lives on in contemporary maker movements, in the renewed appreciation for craft, and in the enduring suspicion that speed and volume are not the only measures of progress.

The Roycroft Movement did not stop industrialization. It did something arguably more difficult. It offered a counterexample. In a time of relentless acceleration, East Aurora proposed deliberation. In a culture obsessed with novelty, Roycroft insisted on durability. In an economy increasingly divorced from meaning, it argued that the hand, the heart, and the hammer could still belong to the same human story.

For Buffalo and Western New York, Roycroft remains a reminder that innovation does not always mean faster or bigger. Sometimes it means better. Sometimes it means choosing to make things, and lives, with care.

Built to Move the World

Buffalo and the Legacy of the Automobile

From the moment the first horseless carriages rattled over Buffalo's smooth streets in the late 1890s, the city seemed destined to become an automotive powerhouse. It had everything a young industry could want. Power from Niagara. Deep water and rail lines that stitched together continents. Skilled craftsmen shaped by iron, wood, and steam. Early, well-maintained roads that made motoring practical rather than theatrical. By every rational measure, Buffalo should have become another Detroit.

And yet, it never quite did.

The automotive industry nonetheless played a major role in Buffalo's economy for more than a century, shaping neighborhoods, employing tens of thousands, and producing some of the most respected vehicles and components in the world. Buffalo's automotive story is not one of absence, but of divergence. It is a tale of excellence over scale, pride over pragmatism, and a city that built cars too well, too carefully, and sometimes too expensively for the age of mass production that followed.

They were just too good; the quality was just too high. These words echo through Buffalo's automotive past like the hum of a finely tuned engine idling at a red light, beautifully built, patiently waiting, while traffic rushes past.

Paradise of Smooth Streets

According to the Buffalo and Erie County Historical Society, the horseless carriage first appeared in Buffalo around 1895. By 1902, the city already counted 465 electric, steam, and gasoline-powered vehicles navigating what one observer described as a "paradise of smooth streets." These early automobiles cruised past horses and bicycles at the state speed limit of 8 to 15 miles per hour, a pace that felt thrilling at the time.

What made Buffalo unique was not simply that it adopted the automobile early, but that it built them. Between 1895 and 1950, more than 30 automobile makes were produced in the Buffalo area, most clustered in the first decades of the twentieth century. Many were small, underfinanced, and short-lived, casualties of an industry evolving faster than balance sheets could keep up. Others fell to the unstoppable force of Henry Ford's Model T, introduced in 1908, and the assembly-line revolution of 1913 that made interchangeable parts and low prices the new gospel.

The names of Buffalo's early vehicles now read like a roll call of forgotten ambition: Kensington, Babcock, Conrad, Willet Motor Trucks, Lippard-Stewart, Atterbury, Parenti. Some companies, like the Kensington Automobile Manufacturing Co. (1899–1904), began as bicycle manufacturers, a natural transition at a time when light frames and mechanical ingenuity mattered more than massive factories.

Kensington produced steam and gasoline models and proudly advertised that its Tonneau could travel 150 miles on roughly eight quarts of gasoline at speeds up to 30 miles per hour. The 1903 Conrad touring car, built on Niagara Street, sold for $1,250 and featured a 12-horsepower double-cylinder engine, three forward gears, one reverse, and "wheel steering," a detail worth advertising in an era still experimenting with control.

Buffalo was inventing the automobile as it went, confident that craftsmanship and innovation would carry the day.

The Thomas Flyer and the Glory of Endurance

Few Buffalo-built cars captured the world's imagination like the Thomas Flyer. Produced from 1900 to 1913 at a factory on Niagara Street, on the site now occupied by Rich Products Corp., the Thomas Flyer was rugged, elegant, and unapologetically expensive.

Its defining moment came in 1908, when a Model 35 Thomas Flyer won the New York to Paris auto race. The contest began in Times Square and headed west, across America, with vehicles shipped to Asia after reaching the Pacific. From there, drivers crossed Siberia, sometimes traveling on the Trans-Siberian Railway and sometimes driving across terrain that barely deserved the name "road," moving only when trains were not expected.

Covering 13,341 miles in 170 days, the Thomas Flyer's victory was less about speed than survival. It proved that an automobile built in Buffalo could endure the world's harshest conditions. The win brought international acclaim, but it did not translate into mass-market dominance. The Flyer was admired, not imitated, and admiration does not always pay the bills.

Pierce-Arrow: Luxury, Pride, and Decline

If the Thomas Flyer was Buffalo's global ambassador, Pierce-Arrow was its crown jewel. Produced from 1901 to 1938, Pierce-Arrow automobiles emerged from a massive plant at Elmwood and Great Arrow in North Buffalo, a building that still stands as an industrial cathedral. At its peak, more than 10,000 people worked there, in what was reputed to be the largest auto plant in the world at the time.

They started with iceboxes and bird cages before George Pierce built his first automobile, the Motorette, in 1901. Pierce-Arrows quickly developed a reputation for durability and refinement, routinely winning long-distance endurance races in an era before paved roads were common.

Presidents and royalty took notice. In 1913, President William Howard Taft purchased a Pierce-Arrow, and in 1930 the company made headlines by building a $20,000 custom vehicle for the Shah of Persia. Pierce-Arrow did not

1908 -Model 35 Thomas Flyer

chase customers. Customers sought Pierce-Arrow.

But by the 1920s, competition in the luxury market intensified. While rivals diversified and adopted mass production techniques, Pierce-Arrow executives clung to the belief that their cars existed above competition. They built only luxury vehicles, resisted assembly-line efficiencies, and dismissed the appeal of lower-priced models.

Studebaker purchased Pierce-Arrow in 1928, and in 1933 a management team bought Studebaker itself. The new owners cut prices and adjusted strategy, but the change came too late. In 1938, amid the lingering Great Depression, Federal Judge John Knight ordered the company liquidated. Buffalo lost not just a manufacturer, but a symbol of its belief that excellence alone could triumph over scale.

The Road Not Taken: Henry Ford and Buffalo

Buffalo could have been Detroit. Henry Ford came to Buffalo in the early 1900s for an auto show and wanted to build a major assembly plant in the city. Buffalo's advantages were obvious. It had power, water, skilled craftsmen, a major rail yard, proximity to Canada, access to Europe through the Great Lakes, and good roads early on.

What Buffalo did not offer was incentives.

The city fathers declined to make concessions, and Ford went elsewhere. Elsewhere was Detroit, where Ford built the River Rouge complex and reshaped industrial history. Originally from Dearborn, Ford had gone to Detroit in 1879 as a machinist's apprentice, became a mechanical engineer, and built his first automobile there in 1903. Detroit embraced him. Buffalo hesitated.

Despite that decision, Ford became and remains a major presence in Buffalo's automotive landscape. Ford had been assembling vehicles in Buffalo since 1910, operating a facility near Main and Rodney Streets. In 1938, the company opened a much larger assembly plant on Fuhrmann Boulevard at Ohio Street, strategically located on the waterfront for easy loading and unloading by lake freighters.

Over the next 20 years, that plant produced an estimated two million vehicles before closing in 1958. Today, the building belongs to the Niagara Frontier Transportation Authority, a reminder that Buffalo still builds infrastructure, even when the products change.

In 1950, Ford deepened its local footprint by opening the Lackawanna stamping plant, which continues to play a major role in the company's supply chain.

General Motors and the Component City

General Motors entered Buffalo's automotive story in 1923, assembling Chevrolets at a plant

Opposite: Ford Assembly Plant on Fuhrmann Boulevard

on East Delavan Avenue, now operated by American Axle. Production continued until July 31, 1941, when the looming entry of the United States into World War II shifted the plant to defense manufacturing.

After the war, the facility returned to automotive production, this time manufacturing rear axles under GM's Saginaw Division. The operation was eventually spun off to American Axle, reinforcing Buffalo's role as a component powerhouse rather than a brand city.

GM's Town of Tonawanda facility, now part of its Powertrain Group, has produced engines and components since 1938 under various names. GM's influence extended to Lockport as well, through Delphi Harrison Thermal Systems, whose roots trace back to 1910 when Herbert Harrison built his first automotive radiator in a small shop.

Buffalo, it turned out, excelled not just at building cars, but at building the things cars depend on.

Tires, Wipers, and the Details That Matter

Two other automotive giants left deep tracks in Buffalo. Dunlop Tire and Rubber established operations in Tonawanda in 1923, long after John Boyd Dunlop invented the pneumatic tire in England in 1888 to smooth his son's bicycle ride. The company continues to produce tires at its original Sheridan Drive and River Road site, now under the ownership of Sumitomo Rubber Industries of Japan.

Trico Products began in 1917, born from a moment of inconvenience on Delaware Avenue. Its founder, John Oishei, struck a pedestrian while driving in the rain, hampered by the absence of windshield wipers. He invented the first hand-operated wiper, and Trico, short for Tri-Continental, was born. At its peak in 1985, Trico employed 2,200 workers across three Buffalo plants. By the early 1990s, most production had moved south, leaving only a shadow of its former presence.

Legacy on Four Wheels

Buffalo's automotive history is not a story of failure. It is a story of choices. The city built cars that conquered continents, vehicles fit for presidents and shahs, and components that powered millions of machines worldwide. It valued quality, endurance, and craftsmanship, sometimes at the expense of speed and scale.

Buffalo did not become Detroit. But it helped build the automotive world all the same, one finely machined part, one overbuilt engine, and one beautifully stubborn idea at a time.

The People's Palace

Buffalo Central Terminal

The Buffalo Central Terminal has long been called the people's palace–and the name fits. Rising from the Broadway-Fillmore neighborhood in 1929, the Buffalo Central Terminal was not merely a train station. It was a declaration. A 17-story Art Deco masterpiece designed by Fellheimer & Wagner for the New York Central Railroad, it announced that Buffalo was a city of movement, ambition, and architectural confidence.

When it opened on Saturday, June 22, 1929, the celebration matched the scale of the building. The public flooded in–thousands eager to see the magnificence. By midnight, the first of more than 200 daily trains began arriving and departing, including a large number of all-Pullman luxury runs.

At its peak, the Terminal handled more than 10,000 passengers daily. It was engineered with precision for movement, designed to keep arriving and departing travelers separate, accommodating as many as 3,200 people per hour.

The octagonal tower became the station's defining landmark. Fifteen stories tall and illuminated at night, it could be seen from fifteen miles away. Four elevators served its offices and public levels, reinforcing the Terminal's role as both transportation hub and business center. Beneath the grand public spaces were three additional levels: track access connected to Curtiss Street and streetcars; baggage and mail handling areas included food storage and dormitories for employees; and below it all lay the basement infrastructure that kept the palace humming.

The concourse spanned fourteen platform tracks, with stairways descending to trains bound for Chicago, New York, and beyond. In 1929 alone, the New York Central Railroad operated 91,420 passenger trains in and out of Buffalo. The Terminal replaced a smaller downtown station and officially opened with the departure of the eastbound Empire State Express. Buffalo had built for the future.

That future surged during World War II. The Buffalo Central Terminal experienced its peak activity during the war years, serving as a critical transport hub for thousands of troops, war material, and civilians. Uniformed soldiers filled the concourse. Red Cross volunteers moved through the crowds. Freight and passenger schedules ran at relentless pace as Buffalo's factories powered the arsenal of democracy. The Terminal became not just a gateway to the West, but a corridor to the front lines. For many young men and women, its marble floors were the last piece of home they saw before boarding trains east or south. For families, the station was a place of tearful departures and anxious reunions.

Yet the postwar decades brought change. Beginning in the 1950s, passenger rail traffic declined nationwide as automobiles and airplanes redefined travel. By 1979, the last train departed. The palace fell silent.

Still, its story did not end. In 1984, the Terminal was placed on both the National and State Registers of Historic Places, recognizing its architectural and cultural significance. Today, restoration efforts continue, driven by volunteers and preservationists determined to revive its grandeur.

Though no longer dispatching 200 trains a day, the Buffalo Central Terminal remains what it has always been: a monument to movement, a landmark of Art Deco ambition, and a symbol of the Broadway-Fillmore neighborhood's enduring spirit.

The Olmsted Park System

Buffalo's Green Blueprint

When Frederick Law Olmsted first turned his attention to Buffalo in the late nineteenth century, he encountered a city at full industrial stride. Grain elevators crowded the harbor, rail lines radiated outward, and new wealth fueled bold architecture and rapid expansion. Buffalo was powerful, ambitious, and growing fast. What it lacked, Olmsted believed, was not energy or confidence, but balance. His solution was neither ornamental nor incidental. It was a comprehensive park system, conceived as civic infrastructure and intended to shape how the city would grow, breathe, and endure.

Working with his longtime partner Calvert Vaux, Olmsted proposed something radical for its time: an interconnected network of parks and parkways designed as a single, coherent system. Rather than isolated green squares dropped into the city as afterthoughts, Buffalo would receive landscapes that guided development, protected public health, and offered daily relief from the pressures of industrial life. In embracing this idea, Buffalo became one of the first American cities to adopt Olmsted's park system philosophy in full.

Parks as Civic Infrastructure

Olmsted did not see parks as luxury amenities. He saw them as essential public works, comparable to streets, water systems, and schools. Landscapes, when carefully planned, could influence social behavior, reduce stress, improve physical health, and create a shared civic identity. Parks were democratic spaces, open to all, where class distinctions softened and citizens encountered one another on equal ground.

Equally important were the connections between parks. The broad, tree-lined parkways were not merely scenic roads. They were linear parks in their own right, designed to slow traffic, frame long vistas, and make movement through the city restorative rather than exhausting. Together, parks and parkways formed a green framework that shaped Buffalo's northward expansion and defined entire neighborhoods.

Delaware Park: The Pastoral Heart

At the center of the system stands Delaware Park, the most expansive and pastoral of Buffalo's Olmsted landscapes. Designed as a democratic countryside within the city, Delaware Park features sweeping meadows, gently curving paths, and the reflective waters of Hoyt Lake. Nothing about the park is accidental. The contours of the land, the placement of trees, and the sightlines across open grass were carefully engineered to appear natural while encouraging calm, contemplation, and informal recreation.

Delaware Park was intended to be experienced slowly. Visitors walking or riding through the park were meant to feel removed from the city's noise without ever leaving it. Over time, the park became a focal point for civic life, hosting gatherings, leisure activities, and quiet daily use that reinforced Olmsted's belief in the restorative power of shared green space.

Humboldt Park: Formality and Order

To the east, Humboldt Park provided a counterpoint to Delaware Park's pastoral character. Humboldt Park featured more formal arrangements, with axial paths, open lawns, and structured plantings. It was designed to serve surrounding neighborhoods while anchoring the eastern reach of the park system.

Though smaller in scale, Humboldt Park played a crucial role in demonstrating Olmsted's belief that every district deserved access to thoughtfully designed open space. The park was not reserved for elites or special occasions. It was woven into everyday neighborhood life, reinforcing the idea that parks should be as accessible as sidewalks.

Opposite: Delaware Park Casino/Boathouse -1901

Front Park: The City Meets the Water

Front Park, overlooking Lake Erie and the Niagara River, connected the park system to Buffalo's maritime identity. Unlike the inward-looking calm of Delaware Park, Front Park embraced expansive views and open horizons. It reminded visitors of Buffalo's position as a gateway city, shaped by water and movement.

Front Park also served a symbolic function. By placing a major public park along the waterfront, Olmsted and Vaux reinforced the idea that natural beauty and public access should not be sacrificed to industry alone. Even in a working port city, the shoreline could remain a shared civic asset.

The Parkways: Green Corridors of Movement

The parks were bound together by a network of parkways that gave the system its coherence. Bidwell Parkway, Lincoln Parkway, and Chapman Parkway were designed as wide, landscaped corridors that extended the park experience into daily travel.

Homes along these parkways benefited from protected green frontage, while travelers experienced long, uninterrupted views framed by trees. These routes discouraged commercial intrusion and heavy traffic, preserving their role as civic promenades rather than utilitarian roads. In this way, Olmsted's system influenced not only where Buffalo built parks, but how it built neighborhoods.

Health, Democracy, and Social Vision

Underlying every design decision was Olmsted's belief in the social value of landscape. Parks were antidotes to the crowding, pollution, and mental strain of industrial cities. They offered physical exercise, fresh air, and visual relief. Just as importantly, they fostered social mixing. In a park, factory workers, merchants, and professionals occupied the same benches and paths.

Buffalo's leaders understood this vision and supported it with unusual consistency. The park system became a point of civic pride, a visible expression of the city's confidence that progress and humanity could coexist.

Decline, Rediscovery, and Renewal

Like many American cities, Buffalo's park system suffered during the mid-twentieth century. The rise of the automobile transformed parkways into commuter routes. Deferred maintenance dulled landscapes carefully tuned to subtle effects. Some parks lost clarity as original design intentions were obscured.

Yet the system never collapsed. Its bones were too strong. In recent decades, renewed attention to Olmsted's work sparked restoration efforts aimed at recovering original layouts, reestablishing historic plantings, and rebalancing parkways as shared civic spaces. Preservationists and planners recognized that these landscapes were not relics, but living systems capable of adaptation.

A Living Legacy

Today, the Olmsted Park System remains one of Buffalo's most profound achievements. It shapes how residents move through the city, where neighborhoods gather, and how nature is experienced in daily life. Joggers follow paths laid out more than a century ago. Children play beneath trees planted with deliberate foresight. Commuters pass through corridors designed to calm rather than rush.

More than a collection of parks, the system represents a philosophy made physical. It reflects the belief that cities thrive when nature is integrated rather than ornamental, and when public space is planned with the same seriousness as commerce or industry. In Buffalo, Olmsted's green blueprint did more than beautify the city. It gave it resilience, coherence, and room to breathe.

Delaware Park Bridge

Buffalo's Built Environment

How Grain, Rails, and Money Quietly Summoned Architectural Giants to Buffalo

Buffalo did not accidentally attract world-class architects. It recruited them without ever sending an invitation.

In the late nineteenth and early twentieth centuries, the city sat astride one of the most lucrative choke points in North America. Grain flowed east from the Midwest. Coal and manufactured goods moved west. Rail lines converged. Lake boats queued up like patient draft horses. Every transfer of cargo created friction, and every bit of friction created money. Buffalo learned how to monetize that moment when one form of transportation had to shake hands with another.

The wealth that followed was not flashy at first. It was industrial money. Transactional money. Quiet money that piled up in ledgers rather than ballrooms. But over time, that wealth began to look for expression. And when money looks for expression, it eventually turns to architecture.

This is how a city built on grain dust and steel rails became a proving ground for giants like Frank Lloyd Wright, H. H. Richardson, and Louis Sullivan.

Buffalo's grain economy created more than silos. It created systems. Elevators had to be engineered, financed, insured, and managed. Railroads required terminals, offices, hotels, and warehouses. Entire corporate ecosystems grew around moving commodities a few feet at a time. That ecosystem produced a new class of clients. Not aristocrats. Not old-money patrons. Industrialists, bankers, insurers, and executives who wanted buildings that signaled seriousness, permanence, and modernity.

These clients were not chasing ornament for ornament's sake. They wanted architecture that matched their self-image. Rational, confident, forward-looking. That desire aligned perfectly with a generation of architects eager to break from borrowed European styles and invent something American.

Take H. H. Richardson. His Romanesque work, heavy with stone and authority, resonated with Buffalo's industrial elite. Richardson's buildings

Above: The Darwin D. Martin House- Frank Lloyd Wright – built between 1903 and 1905.
Opposite: Guaranty Building,/ Prudential Building, Louis Sullivan and Dankmar Adler –1896.

looked like they could withstand pressure, financial and otherwise. Thick walls. Deep arches. A sense of gravity. For men whose fortunes depended on infrastructure that could not fail, this language made sense. Buffalo's wealth did not want lace. It wanted load-bearing confidence.

Richardson arrived not because Buffalo chased him, but because Buffalo spoke his language. The city's money had already decided what kind of architecture it respected.

Louis Sullivan followed a similar gravitational pull, though his philosophy pointed toward the future rather than mass. Sullivan believed that form should follow function, an idea that fit neatly into a city obsessed with efficiency. Grain elevators themselves were radical functional objects. Tall, cylindrical, unapologetically utilitarian. Engineers built them before architects realized how modern they were. Sullivan's work translated that industrial honesty into civic and commercial buildings. He did not hide structure. He celebrated it.

Buffalo's financiers understood this instinctively. They lived inside systems where efficiency was profit. They were willing to fund architecture that looked different because their wealth was built on doing things differently. The city's economic engine made it intellectually hospitable to architectural innovation.

Then there is Frank Lloyd Wright, whose relationship with Buffalo was both personal and professional. Wright arrived young, ambitious,

H. H. Richardson - Buffalo Psychiatric Center complex, originally called the State Asylum for the Insane, built 1870-1871

and searching for patrons who would let him experiment. Buffalo had them. The city's grain and rail fortunes had matured into generational wealth, and with maturity came a willingness to take risks on ideas rather than just assets.

Wright's Buffalo clients were not interested in replicas of the past. They wanted something that matched their sense of arrival. Prairie lines, open plans, integrated design. Wright's work offered a vision of American life that felt self-confident and unborrowed. Buffalo, flush with capital yet distant from East Coast social hierarchies, was fertile ground for that vision.

What is often missed is that this patronage was indirect. Grain barons did not wake up wanting architectural revolutions. They wanted offices, homes, and institutions that reflected their success. The revolution happened because the money came with fewer cultural strings attached. Buffalo's wealth was earned through logistics, not lineage. That made it more open to new ideas.

Railroads amplified this effect. Rail companies were among the largest corporations of their era. They required standardized systems, clear branding, and architectural presence across multiple cities. Buffalo, as a rail hub, became a place where corporate architecture mattered. Stations, headquarters, and related buildings had to communicate order and progress. Architects who could think systemically had an advantage.

The city's role as a transfer point also meant constant exposure. Executives, engineers, and investors passed through Buffalo daily. They saw its buildings. They noticed its ambition. Architecture became part of the city's business card.

There is also a subtler factor. Grain and rail wealth concentrated capital geographically. Unlike dispersed agricultural profits, this money accumulated in offices and banks clustered downtown. That density made large commissions possible. Architects were not designing one building at a time. They were shaping districts. That scale attracted talent.

By the early twentieth century, Buffalo had something rare. Capital, confidence, and clients willing to commission ideas rather than copies. Wright, Richardson, and Sullivan did not just build in Buffalo. They tested ideas there. They refined philosophies. They left behind work that influenced their broader careers.

None of this diminishes the importance of local architects who filled in the city between the icons. But it explains why the icons came at all. Buffalo's industrial economy created the conditions. Grain paid for stone. Rails financed innovation. Elevators funded experimentation.

The irony is that the same forces that later contributed to Buffalo's economic challenges were the ones that once made it a laboratory for American architecture. Infrastructure wealth is cyclical. But architecture endures.

When you stand in Buffalo today and admire a building by one of these giants, you are also looking at grain contracts, rail schedules, insurance tables, and balance sheets made solid. The money moved on. The architecture stayed.

That is the quiet alchemy of cities. Commerce builds the stage. Architecture remembers the moment when everything briefly aligned.

Buffalo's skyline likes to take bows for its celebrities.

Say the names Frank Lloyd Wright, H. H. Richardson, or Louis Sullivan and even casual architecture fans nod along. The trinity deserves its applause. Their buildings are pilgrimage sites. They anchor textbooks. They give tour guides something dramatic to point at while buses idle.

But a city does not live on icons alone.

Cities are not museums. They are ecosystems. They are stitched together by schools and offices, hospitals and homes, factories and storefronts. They are shaped less by monuments than by repetition. By the reliable hand that shows up again and again, block after block, decade after decade, quietly making a place work. In Buffalo, that work was done by local architects who rarely get top billing but whose fingerprints are everywhere. If the famous names gave Buffalo its punctuation marks, these builders wrote the paragraphs.

Start with Louise Blanchard Bethune, because every city needs at least one pioneer who forces the door open. Bethune was not just Buffalo's first prominent woman architect. She was the first woman in the United States to open her own architectural practice. That fact alone should stop traffic. Yet Bethune's legacy is not about novelty. It is about competence at scale. Schools, factories, office buildings, churches. She designed them to be used, not admired from velvet ropes. Her buildings said something radical for their time: permanence was not a male trait. Buffalo trusted her with its future, brick by brick.

Then there is Edward Brodhead Green, whose partnership with William Sydney Wicks would quietly define huge swaths of the city. Green understood something essential about Buffalo's moment. This was a city building fast, fueled by industry and ambition, but also aware of its climate and character. His work balanced elegance with endurance. These were buildings that could take a Lake Erie winter on the chin and still look respectable come spring. No small feat.

Speaking of Wicks, William Sydney Wicks deserves his own spotlight. Where others chased stylistic statements, Wicks specialized in coherence. His designs understood context before context was a buzzword. They fit their neighborhoods the way a good sentence fits a paragraph. You do not notice them at first. Then you realize the whole block works because of them.

That sense of urban grammar also defines Green & Wicks. Together, Green and Wicks shaped Buffalo's civic confidence. Their buildings project authority without arrogance. They feel trustworthy. Banks, schools, public buildings. Places where people needed to believe the system would hold. Architecture as reassurance.

Earlier still, August Esenwein and James A. Johnson were laying down Buffalo's late nineteenth-century backbone. Their partnership gave the city a muscular, forward-looking look just as it was stepping onto the national stage. These were buildings that signaled arrival. Not

Above: Buffalo and Erie County Botanical Gardens - Lord & Burnham 1894-1900
Opposite: Seneca One Tower/Marine Midland Center - Gordon Bunshaft -1972

M&T Bank

flashy, not timid. Confident. They told the world Buffalo was not passing through its own history. It was settling in.

Another local master of tone was George Cary, who had the rare ability to design buildings that felt both cultured and accessible. Cary's work borrowed classical language without slipping into imitation. His buildings speak softly but fluently. They do not shout their lineage. They assume you'll understand.

Buffalo's story would be incomplete without Lord & Burnham, whose structures remind us that architecture is not always about walls. Their conservatories and greenhouses were feats of engineering as much as design. They brought light and life indoors, even in winter. In a city defined by cold months, that mattered. They gave Buffalo places to breathe.

And then there is Gordon Bunshaft, often remembered for his modernist work elsewhere, but still part of Buffalo's extended architectural family. Bunshaft represents a bridge. Between old Buffalo and new. Between masonry confidence and glass ambition. His work suggests a city willing to evolve without erasing itself.

Beverly (Bonnie)Foit-Albert

Rounding out the roster is Beverly Foit-Albert, whose legacy is measured not in skylines altered but in skylines protected. Preservation, after all, is architecture's second heartbeat. It calls for discipline over ego, patience over spectacle, and a reverence for the hands that built before us.

Foit-Albert helped Buffalo recognize that its history was not excess baggage to be discarded, but capital quietly accruing value. In a city famous for its architectural inheritance, Foit-Albert's work reminds us that preservation is not nostalgia. It is stewardship. And stewardship, done well, becomes a form of quiet courage.

What unites all of these architects is not a shared style. It is a shared ethic. They built for Buffalo as it actually was, not as a concept sketch. They designed for workers and students, patients and parishioners. For people who would use the buildings every day, not just admire them once.

Their work explains why Buffalo still feels like a city that knows itself. Walk its neighborhoods and you sense continuity. The scale holds. The streets make sense. The buildings feel invested in their blocks. That does not happen by accident. It happens when local architects understand local lives.

So yes, celebrate the giants. Bring visitors to the icons. Print the postcards. But if you want to understand Buffalo, look beyond the landmarks. Look at the schools that still open their doors every morning. The offices that have outlasted entire industries. The hospitals, churches, and homes that quietly kept going.

That is where Buffalo's real architectural story lives. Not in isolated masterpieces, but in the steady, collective work of local hands that built a city sturdy enough to endure and flexible enough to adapt. A city that, even now, stands on the confidence they poured into its foundations.

General Electric Tower - James A. Johnson and built in 1912.

Kleinhans Music Hall

Modernism, Music, and a City That Listens

Kleinhans Music Hall

Modernism, Music, and a City That Listens

Few buildings in Buffalo express the city's cultural confidence as clearly as Kleinhans Music Hall. Opened in 1940, the hall is both an architectural landmark and a living performance space, internationally respected for its acoustics and admired for its restraint. Where other concert halls lean toward ornament, Kleinhans chose clarity. The result is a building that lets the music speak first.

Designed by Finnish architect Eliel Saarinen, with contributions from his son Eero Saarinen, Kleinhans represents a pivotal moment in modern architecture. Its clean lines, flowing curves, and warm materials broke sharply from classical concert hall design. This was modernism made humane, a structure that felt progressive without being cold. For Buffalo, commissioning Saarinen signaled an outward-looking ambition, a belief that the city belonged in international cultural conversations.

The hall exists because of philanthropy rooted in local life. Edward L. Kleinhans and his wife Mary Seaton Kleinhans left a bequest specifically to create a home for music in Buffalo. Their gift was not abstract. It was practical, civic-minded, and enduring. Kleinhans Music Hall stands as a reminder that private generosity can leave public legacy when aligned with shared values.

At the heart of the building is the Buffalo Philharmonic Orchestra, which has called Kleinhans home since its opening. The

relationship between hall and orchestra is symbiotic. The BPO's sound helped define the hall's reputation, while the hall's acoustics elevated the orchestra's performance. Musicians and conductors routinely praise the space for its warmth, balance, and intimacy. Notes carry without strain. Silence matters as much as sound.

Over the decades, Kleinhans has hosted far more than symphonic music. Jazz legends, soloists, choral ensembles, and visiting orchestras have all taken the stage. The hall's flexibility allowed it to remain relevant even as musical tastes shifted. While trends came and went, the building's purpose stayed constant: focused listening.

Kleinhans also occupies a distinctive place in Buffalo's urban fabric. Located just west of downtown, it anchors a residential neighborhood rather than a commercial strip. Concert nights feel communal. Audiences arrive on foot, greet neighbors, and disperse quietly afterward. The experience reinforces the idea that culture does not need spectacle to matter.

Preservation has played a critical role in Kleinhans' longevity. Designated a National Historic Landmark, the hall has undergone careful restoration to maintain its original character while updating infrastructure. These efforts reflect an understanding that architectural integrity and functional relevance are not opposing goals, but complementary ones.

In a city that has wrestled repeatedly with questions of identity and value, Kleinhans Music Hall offers a steady answer. It embodies patience, craftsmanship, and trust in audiences. It assumes that people will sit still, listen closely, and return for more.

Kleinhans does not shout its importance. It resonates. In doing so, it reminds Buffalo that some of its strongest cultural statements are made not through reinvention, but through sustained excellence.

Forest Lawn Cemetery

Where Buffalo's History Comes to Rest

More than a burial ground, Forest Lawn Cemetery is one of Buffalo's most revealing civic landscapes, a place where memory and design hold quiet conversation beneath a canopy of trees. Founded in 1849, Forest Lawn embraced a nineteenth century notion that still feels gently rebellious: a cemetery could be beautiful, contemplative, even social. It could serve the living as faithfully as it honors the dead..

Set along Delaware Avenue, the cemetery unfolds like a curated woodland. Curving drives replace rigid grids. Mature trees frame long sightlines. Monuments rise organically from the terrain rather than crowding shoulder to shoulder. This was deliberate. Mid nineteenth century urban churchyards were cramped and unsanitary. Rural cemeteries offered air, space, and perspective. In Buffalo, Forest Lawn quickly became a destination for Sunday carriage rides, picnics, and contemplative walks. Decades before Frederick Law Olmsted's park system reshaped the city, Forest Lawn functioned as one of Buffalo's earliest public green spaces.

The land itself carries an earlier chapter. In 1806, Erastus Granger, one of Buffalo's most prominent early residents, purchased the property that would later become the cemetery. His ownership ties the site to the city's frontier origins, long before it became a landscaped sanctuary.

Forest Lawn also operates as a ledger of civic life. Industrialists, politicians, artists, soldiers, and everyday citizens rest side by side. Among them is Millard Fillmore, the thirteenth President of the United States. His grave draws visitors from far beyond Buffalo, yet he is only one voice in a vast chorus. The names etched in stone mirror street signs, institutions, and neighborhoods still familiar today. Walking the grounds feels less like touring a cemetery and more like turning the pages of a three dimensional history.

Art and architecture are central to that experience. Mausoleums, obelisks, angels, and relief sculptures chart changing tastes across generations. Some monuments announce wealth with marble bravado. Others whisper with spare intimacy. Collectively, they reveal how Buffalo understood faith, status, grief, and permanence. The roster of designers reads like a syllabus in American art and architecture: Stanford White, Augustus Saint-Gaudens, E. B. Green, Richard Upjohn, N. Cantalamessa-Papotti, George Cary, Charles Cary Rumsey, and Frank Lloyd Wright. Their contributions reinforce that Forest Lawn is as much a cultural campus as a funerary ground.

Its placement along Delaware Avenue situates the cemetery within Buffalo's grand historic corridor, visually and symbolically linked to nearby cultural institutions and parkland. People pass its gates in the course of ordinary days, reminded that the city's present stands directly atop its past. Families continue to choose it as a resting place, and careful stewardship balances preservation with contemporary needs. Guided tours, history walks, and educational programs invite visitors to engage with the grounds as a place of learning. Tragedies of epidemics, wars, industrial accidents, and economic upheavals are recorded here alongside triumphs, offering a sober counterpoint to Buffalo's architectural bravado.

In a city celebrated for reinvention, Forest Lawn offers something steadier. It reminds Buffalo that progress is cumulative, built by lives that end but leave fingerprints everywhere. Its winding paths slow the pace. Its monuments ask questions. Forest Lawn endures because it fulfills its original promise: a place where landscape, memory, and civic identity meet, and where history is not sealed away, but allowed to breathe.

SCHICKEL

Between Silence and Survival

Buffalo's German Americans Through Two World Wars

Before World War I, Buffalo ranked among the most German cities in the United States. German immigrants and their descendants shaped neighborhoods, filled churches and social halls, dominated skilled trades, and built much of the city's brewing and industrial base. In parts of the East Side, German was not a foreign language but the language of daily life. That visibility, once a source of confidence and cohesion, would become a liability once war reshaped public sentiment.

A powerful symbol of that prewar presence stood at 424 Main Street, at the corner of Court Street. Founded in 1882, the German American Bank was one of five Buffalo banks capitalized with German investment. Its location, scale, and clientele reflected a community that was prosperous, organized, and confident in its place within the city. The bank was more than a financial institution; it was a civic marker of belonging.

World War I changed that almost overnight. When the United States entered the war in 1917, German Americans in Buffalo faced -suspicion that cut across class and generation. Long-established families were suddenly asked to prove loyalty that had once been assumed. Surveillance increased. Harassment was common. Cultural expression became risky.

The war hastened a broader collapse of ethnic identification with the old country, not just in Buffalo but across the nation. German-language newspapers closed or sharply reduced publication. Schools eliminated German instruction. Public use of the language faded rapidly as families chose safety over tradition. Even everyday words became suspect. In 1918, amid sharp and emotional backlash, hamburger was rechristened "Salisbury steak," dachshunds became "liberty pups," and German music, literature, and club life retreated from public view.

Businesses moved quickly to adapt. Names, signage, and branding were scrubbed of German associations. The most prominent example was the German American Bank, which became Liberty Bank in 1918. The change was both symbolic and strategic, a declaration of loyalty in an atmosphere where neutrality was no longer acceptable. What had once been a proud ethnic identifier was recast as a potential threat.

The transformation did not stop at a name. The original bank structure was eventually torn down, and in its place rose a new statement of American identity. Completed in 1925, the 23-story Liberty Bank tower reshaped Buffalo's skyline. The building did not simply blend in; it overcompensated. Crowning the structure were two reduced-scale replicas of Bartholdi's Statue of Liberty, unmistakable symbols of patriotism and allegiance. Architecture became reassurance. Stone and steel spoke where words might invite doubt.

By the end of World War I, Buffalo's visible German culture had been dismantled with remarkable speed. What had once been celebrated publicly moved indoors, into kitchens, family gatherings, and private memory. The scars of that period lingered.

When World War II arrived, the lessons of the earlier conflict were already absorbed. German Americans were, by then, deeply assimilated, and cultural visibility was approached cautiously.

While German nationals were again subject to loyalty checks and enemy-alien classifications, the repression was less explosive than during World War I. Even so, memory enforced restraint. Families avoided public displays of heritage. Silence became a form of self-preservation.

Yet contribution never ceased. German Americans remained embedded in Buffalo's industrial workforce, staffing factories, machine shops, and construction sites essential to wartime production. The brewing industry, long shaped by German skill and tradition, continued to anchor the local economy, even as its cultural roots went largely unspoken. German Americans served in uniform, worked defense jobs, and participated fully in civic life, proving loyalty through labor rather than language.

Together, the two world wars reshaped Buffalo's German-American community in lasting ways. A once highly visible culture receded into private space. Identity survived, but quietly. Traditions were preserved without banners. Pride endured without parades.

Buffalo's German Americans did not disappear; they adapted. Like the Liberty Bank tower itself, they stood tall while learning when not to call attention to their foundations. Their influence remains woven into the city's neighborhoods, industries, craftsmanship, and skyline, a legacy shaped as much by restraint as by achievement.

Liberty Bank Building

Shadows at the Margins

The Ku Klux Klan in Buffalo

Buffalo's history is most often told through stories of labor, immigration, and civic resilience. Yet, like many American cities in the early twentieth century, it also encountered darker undercurrents. Among them was the brief but revealing presence of the Ku Klux Klan during the 1920s. Though never dominant in Western New York, the Klan's appearance exposed how national movements of fear and exclusion could surface even in cities built by immigrants and organized labor.

The post–World War I Klan, revived nationally in 1915, differed markedly from its Reconstruction-era predecessor. It rebranded itself as a "patriotic" fraternal organization, cloaking intolerance in the language of morality and Americanism. Its targets expanded beyond African Americans to include Catholics, Jews, immigrants, labor organizers, and anyone labeled insufficiently loyal or "un-American." This message gained traction in a nation unsettled by Prohibition, labor unrest, rapid immigration, and cultural change. Buffalo, with its dense mix of Irish, Italian, Jewish, Polish, and German communities, embodied precisely the pluralism that provoked Klan hostility.

In the early 1920s, the Klan operated in Buffalo with a combination of secrecy and spectacle. It maintained offices on Chippewa Street, operating out of the Calumet Building on West Chippewa Street. The space was rented through the Kay-Bee Adsign Company, a Klan front designed to conceal the organization's presence in the heart of the city's entertainment district. Recruitment focused primarily on native-born white Protestants who felt culturally or economically displaced by Buffalo's immigrant-majority neighborhoods.

The Klan's most visible demonstration occurred in May 1923, when roughly 200 members were initiated in a field near Buffalo beneath a large, burning cross. While such rituals were less frequent in Western New York than in other regions, the symbolism was unmistakable. The display was intended to project power, inspire loyalty, and intimidate those the Klan viewed as outsiders.

Politically, the Buffalo Klan sought influence rather than outright control. It promoted strict enforcement of Prohibition, attempted to shape school policy, and advanced explicitly anti-Catholic rhetoric aimed squarely at Buffalo's sizable Irish and Italian populations. These efforts intersected with broader social conflicts, particularly labor organizing. The Klan portrayed unions and immigrant workers as threats to moral and social order, positioning itself as a defender of stability during a period of rapid change. Its claims to respectability, however, were met with skepticism in a city long accustomed to coalition politics and ethnic coexistence.

Opposition was swift, organized, and unusually public. Mayor Frank X. Schwab, himself a Catholic and openly opposed to Prohibition, became a prime target of Klan attacks. Schwab did not retreat. In one dramatic episode, he personally confronted armed, hooded Klansmen at a local meeting, signaling that Buffalo's civic leadership would not legitimize intimidation disguised as patriotism.

Schwab's opposition went beyond symbolism. He recruited undercover Buffalo police officer Edward Obertean to infiltrate the Klan. Operating from within the organization, Obertean supplied intelligence directly to the mayor, giving city officials rare insight into Klan operations, membership, and plans. By the summer of 1924, battle lines were clearly drawn, as anti-Klan efforts coalesced around groups such as the United Sons of America and the Liberty League.

The confrontation reached a turning point on July 3, 1924, when Klan headquarters on Chippewa Street were ransacked and internal records stolen. The membership list, containing the names of nearly 4,000 Buffalonians and reflecting additional strength in neighboring Niagara County, soon landed in police hands. Authorities placed the list on public display at police headquarters. Thousands of Buffalonians reportedly lined up to read the names, identifying friends, neighbors, coworkers, and civic leaders. Many listed members quickly distanced themselves from the organization, resigning or denying involvement.

Those records, now digitized by the Buffalo History Museum, proved devastating. The exposure shattered the Klan's secrecy, triggered intense internal dissension, and stripped the organization of its aura of power. Leaders turned on one another, recruitment collapsed, and public ridicule replaced fear.

The conflict turned deadly on August 31, 1924. Thomas Austin, a Klan investigator sent from Atlanta to examine the breach, confronted Obertean outside 128 Durham Street after suspecting his role in the infiltration. The encounter escalated into an exchange of gunfire that killed both men. Obertean's death marked the only fatality directly tied to Buffalo's battle against the Klan. He remains largely unrecognized, despite his role as a key figure in dismantling the organization from within.

By the late 1920s, the Klan had largely vanished from Buffalo's civic life. National scandals, economic uncertainty, and relentless local opposition hastened its collapse. The significance of this episode lies less in the Klan's presence than in its failure. Buffalo's experience demonstrated the strength of civic leadership, organized labor, law enforcement, and community institutions willing to confront exclusion directly. It stands as a reminder that intolerance can surface anywhere, but so can effective resistance when vigilance, solidarity, and courage prevail.

The Queen Grew Wings

Long before jets stitched contrails across the sky, human beings stared upward with a mixture of envy and audacity. The dream of flight flickered through myth and sketchbook, from Leonardo's notebooks to fragile gliders skimming windy dunes. In 1903, the Wright Brothers coaxed powered flight into reality at Kitty Hawk, and the twentieth century tilted permanently skyward.

Within a decade, Buffalo, New York, was no longer merely a canal city or industrial powerhouse. It was an aviation capital.

The Curtiss Revolution

At the center stood Glenn Curtiss, a motorcycle builder from Hammondsport whose mechanical curiosity turned toward wings in the early 1900s. By 1908, Curtiss was the only person in the world focused squarely on developing a commercial aircraft. History often spotlights the Wright Brothers, yet many aviation historians argue that Curtiss did as much, and in some respects more, to transform flight from novelty into industry.

When World War I erupted, Curtiss relocated operations to Buffalo, drawn by its industrial muscle, rail access, and skilled workforce. At 2050 Elmwood Avenue, the Curtiss Aeroplane and Motor Company established what became the largest airplane plant in the world. During the war, Curtiss built roughly 10,000 aircraft in Buffalo alone.

Among them was the legendary Curtiss JN-4 "Jenny," the first mass produced airplane. The Jenny became the classroom of the sky. During World War I, 95 percent of Allied pilots learned to fly on it, including figures such as Eddie Rickenbacker, Amelia Earhart, and Charles Lindbergh. The Jenny democratized flight, turning daredevil spectacle into standardized training.

Curtiss innovation did not stop there. In Buffalo, engineers developed the first flying boat and the first aircraft to take off from a ship. After the war, the company built the NC-4, the first aircraft to cross the Atlantic in 1919, proving that oceans were obstacles, not barriers.

By that point, Buffalo was arguably the largest aircraft manufacturing center in the world.

An Airport and an Industry

The 1920s carried aviation from military necessity into civilian life. Inspired by Curtiss's momentum, city leaders backed construction of

Above: The Curtiss JN-4 "Jenny"
Opposite: Glenn Curtiss

the Buffalo Municipal Airport in Cheektowaga in 1926. Beginning with 318 acres and later expanding to nearly 1,000, it evolved into today's Buffalo Niagara International Airport. Passenger service and airmail routes began in 1927, capitalizing on Buffalo's strategic location between New York City and the Midwest.

Other firms soon joined the ecosystem. Consolidated Aircraft operated out of the old Curtiss plant, developing PBY flying boats before relocating to San Diego. In 1935, Lawrence Bell founded Bell Aircraft Corporation in Buffalo. The city's aviation cluster was no accident. It was industrial gravity at work.

Arsenal of the Air

World War II transformed Buffalo into a roaring cog in the American war machine. Curtiss-Wright expanded operations near the airport, producing 17,575 aircraft during the war, including the formidable P-40 Warhawk. The Curtiss C-46 Commando, at its debut in 1940 the largest twin engine airplane in the world, became a critical military transport.

Bell Aircraft pushed technological frontiers even further. In total secrecy, on an upper floor of what is now the Tri-Main Building, engineers built the Bell P-59 Airacomet, the first jet fighter developed in the United States. Its maiden flight took place on October 2, 1942. Though its performance fell short of expectations, it yielded essential data for future jet development.

Bell also developed the nation's first helicopter in 1943. During the Korean War, Bell helicopters rescued more than 50,000 Allied and American soldiers. Buffalo engineers were not merely building machines. They were altering the geometry of rescue and warfare.

From Sound Barrier to Space

After the wars, aircraft demand cooled, and many companies consolidated. Yet Buffalo's aerospace ingenuity did not fade. Bell engineers developed the Agena rocket engine in the 1960s, powering upper stage rockets that carried early U.S. spacecraft toward the moon, Mars, and Venus. Bell also built the Lunar Landing Training Vehicle simulator that helped prepare astronauts for moon landings. Neil Armstrong later credited the simulator's precision as critical to the success of Apollo 11 in 1969.

Buffalo's aviation story had leapt from wood and canvas to the edge of space.

Flight Today

Large scale aircraft assembly eventually moved elsewhere, but aerospace expertise remains rooted in Western New York. Moog Inc. manufactures flight control systems used by Boeing and Airbus, with components on nearly every commercial and military aircraft flying today. Calspan, formerly the Cornell Aeronautical Laboratory, leads in wind tunnel testing and in flight simulation, shaping aircraft design worldwide.

The region's aviation legacy is preserved and celebrated by the Niagara Aerospace Museum, which curates the artifacts and stories of a century in the sky.

Thc history of flight is often told as a coastal tale, from Kitty Hawk to Cape Canaveral. Yet between those horizons stands Buffalo, a city that once built wings by the thousands and helped teach the world to fly. In the Queen City, aviation was not a footnote. It was lift itself.

Above: Laurence Bell standing next to a Bell P-59 airplane.
Opposite: Production line for the Curtiss-Wright's P-40, known as the Warhawk, Kittyhawk and Tomahawk.

Forged in Weather and Will

A History of Sports in Buffalo

Sports in Buffalo have never been a sideshow. They are stitched into the city's identity as tightly as steel beams and lake wind. In a place shaped by hard work, harsh winters, and long odds, sports became both escape and declaration–a way for Buffalonians to see their own endurance reflected back at them under lights and on ice.

From its earliest days, Buffalo's geography invited competition. Lake Erie, the Niagara River, and long winters fostered skating, rowing, fishing, and informal games played wherever space allowed. As the city industrialized in the nineteenth century, organized sports followed the rhythm of factory whistles. Teams formed around neighborhoods, trades, and ethnic communities, turning recreation into ritual.

Baseball arrived early and stayed. By the late 1800s Buffalo fielded professional teams, and by the twentieth century the city was firmly a baseball town. That legacy lives on through the Buffalo Bisons, one of the oldest continuously operating minor league franchises in the country. Summer nights at the ballpark became civic punctuation marks–predictable, affordable, and communal. Baseball in Buffalo was never about glamour. It was about continuity.

Football, however, gave Buffalo its most enduring stage–and its most famous cathedral of grit: War Memorial Stadium.

Opened in 1937 as Roesch Memorial Stadium and later renamed War Memorial Stadium, it was never elegant. Built during the Great Depression, the concrete bowl was expanded repeatedly in practical, almost improvised fashion. The upper deck in right field earned it a nickname that stuck for decades: "The Rock Pile." It was loud, cramped, exposed to the elements, and beloved.

When the Buffalo Bills began play in 1960, War Memorial Stadium became their proving ground. Fans sat shoulder to shoulder in biting wind, wrapped in blankets and defiance. The stadium amplified Buffalo's personality–unpretentious, resilient, and stubbornly loyal. It was there that the Bills captured AFL championships in the mid-1960s. It was there that generations learned to endure cold metal benches and colder Decembers.

The Rock Pile was not comfortable. It was not polished. But it was authentic. Visiting teams rarely enjoyed the experience. Buffalo fans turned weather into advantage, noise into intimidation, and scarcity into pride. When the Bills moved to Rich Stadium in 1973, nostalgia for War Memorial only deepened. The concrete may have cracked, but the mythology hardened.

If football gave Buffalo its concrete altar, hockey gave it its frozen heartbeat. When the Buffalo Sabres joined the NHL in 1970, the fit felt inevitable. Hockey matched the climate and temperament: fast, physical, unforgiving. The Sabres' Stanley Cup runs in 1975 and 1999 produced moments of shared ecstasy–and shared agony. None lingers more sharply than the soul-crushing echo of "No Goal" in the 1999 Finals. In Buffalo, that phrase needs no explanation. It remains part of the city's emotional shorthand.

Football carried its own defining scar. The early 1990s saw four consecutive Super Bowl appearances by the Bills–a feat unmatched in NFL history. And yet, the image that persists is "Wide Right." The missed field goal in Super Bowl XXV became a civic scar–painful, unforgettable, unifying. In many cities, such losses fracture loyalty. In Buffalo, they forged it.

Basketball briefly joined the story. The Buffalo

Opposite: War Memorial Stadium "The Rock Pile"

D-District
040
SERVING THE COMMUNITY
14
7051
4983
2380
PREACH
CHRIST

Braves brought the NBA to town in 1970, overlapping with the Sabres' debut. Though competitive and occasionally electrifying, the Braves' relocation in 1978 reinforced a familiar lesson: professional sports survival requires more than passion. Even so, their chapter remains part of Buffalo's layered athletic history.

College and high school sports have always mattered here. Friday night football, packed gymnasiums, and University at Buffalo athletics provided local heroes whose names were spoken in classrooms and at kitchen tables. These games felt intimate. Players were classmates, neighbors, coworkers' children. Victory belonged to the block. Loss did too.

Beyond the major leagues, Buffalo's sports culture flourished in boxing gyms, bowling alleys, rowing clubs, and neighborhood diamonds. The city produced Olympic athletes, champions, and coaches who carried Buffalo's imprint outward. Annual marathons, regattas, and charity tournaments turned sport into civic glue.

What distinguishes Buffalo's sports history is not a trophy case overflowing with championships. It is the relationship between teams and city. Sports here were never mere entertainment. They were mirrors. In uphill battles, fans saw their own lives. In weathered stadiums like the Rock Pile, they saw their own stubbornness. In "No Goal" and "Wide Right," they recognized disappointment without surrender.

Today, modern arenas gleam brighter than War Memorial's concrete ever did. Yet the spirit forged in that rough bowl endures. Buffalo sports are not about dominance. They are about belonging. About showing up when it's cold. About remembering the echoes–and coming back anyway.

Buffalo did not invent loyalty. It built a stadium for it.

Above: The Buffalo Blues were the last Buffalo major league baseball team to play in Buffalo. 1913-1915.
Opposite: The YMCA Buffalo Niagara Turkey Trot is an annual 8K Thanksgiving race.
Established in 1896, it's the oldest continually running public footrace in North America.

WELCOME to the FAMOUS
BROADWAY MARKET

The Buffalo Broadway Market

A Living Immigrant Commons

For more than a century, the Buffalo Broadway Market has stood as one of the city's most vivid expressions of immigrant life. Located at 999 Broadway on Buffalo's East Side, the market has never been merely a place to buy food. It has functioned as a civic commons where language, culture, faith, and commerce collided in full voice.

The market's roots stretch back to the late nineteenth century, when Polish, German, and other Eastern European immigrants settled the surrounding neighborhoods. Many arrived from agrarian backgrounds and brought food traditions shaped by necessity and season: smoked meats, dense breads, pickled vegetables, pastries, and cheeses meant to last through long winters. Informal outdoor vending along Broadway eventually coalesced into a recognized public market, and in 1890 the city constructed an enclosed building to house the growing trade.

By the early twentieth century, the Broadway Market had become the beating heart of Buffalo's East Side. In the 1930s, it was the largest and busiest of the five public markets operated by the City of Buffalo. Its energy was legendary. As the Buffalo Times observed on October 4, 1931:

"No, the market is not a quiet place. In fact, it's noisier than a newspaper editorial room. Or a boiler shop. Oceans of foodstuffs and a babel of tongues. Laughter. Shouting. And invitations to buy."

That description captured more than sound. It reflected a place where Polish, German, Ukrainian, and later Italian voices mingled freely, where shopping was inseparable from conversation and community. Vendors sold not just food, but familiarity. Customers shopped by relationship as much as by price, often returning to the same stall for decades.

The original 1890 market building served the neighborhood for more than sixty years before being replaced in 1956 with the current structure. While modernized, the new building preserved the essential character of the market: crowded aisles, independent vendors, and a rhythm dictated by cultural calendars rather than retail trends.

Seasonality has always defined the Broadway Market's identity. No time is more emblematic than Easter weekend, when thousands descend on the market in a ritual that blends commerce with tradition. The air fills with the smell of kielbasa and fresh bread. Counters overflow with chrusciki, horseradish, dyed eggs, and butter lambs destined for Easter baskets and blessing tables. For many families, a trip to the Broadway Market is not optional; it is how the holiday begins.

Despite neighborhood decline in the mid-to-late twentieth century, the market endured when other public markets vanished. Loyal vendors, multigenerational customers, and cultural memory sustained it through lean years. In recent decades, preservation efforts and renewed investment have helped stabilize the market while allowing new vendors to join long-standing ones.

The Broadway Market survives because it was never simply a building. It is a living record of Buffalo's immigrant past and present, loud, crowded, imperfect, and deeply human. In its aisles, the city's history is not preserved behind glass. It is spoken, tasted, argued over, and carried home in paper bags.

The Rise, Fall, and Reinvention of Downtown Buffalo Retail

From the 1830s onward, a short stretch of Main Street in Buffalo functioned as the city's commercial spine, humming with trade, ambition, and foot traffic. These blocks were busy long before neon signs and escalators arrived. Early storefronts were modest affairs: dry-goods merchants sharing narrow spaces, their windows crowded with bolts of cloth, tinware, boots, and household necessities. Living quarters often sat directly above the shop floor, blurring the line between commerce and daily life. This mix of retail, residence, and warehouse activity made lower Main Street a place where Buffalo quite literally lived on top of its economy.

19th-Century Origins *(1830s-1890s)*

As Buffalo grew from frontier village to canal city, retail followed the flow of people and money. Specialized shops clustered along Main Street, close to the docks, the Erie Canal terminus, and later the railroads. Grocers, tailors, jewelers, booksellers, and furniture dealers appeared alongside warehouses that fed both local demand and regional trade. These businesses were largely independent, owner-operated, and intensely competitive. Storefronts were narrow but deep, designed to maximize inventory rather than spectacle.

The construction of the Market Arcade in 1892 marked a turning point. With its iron-and-glass design, the Arcade reflected a growing confidence in downtown as a destination rather than merely a place of necessity. It gathered multiple retailers under one roof, encouraged strolling and browsing, and hinted at a more modern retail experience. By the end of the 19th century, Main Street had become not just a place to buy things, but a place to be seen.

The Golden Age of Department Stores *(Early-Mid 20th Century)*

The early 20th century ushered in downtown Buffalo's retail golden age. Independent shops still thrived, but they were increasingly overshadowed by large, locally owned department stores that transformed shopping into an event. Main Street became a regional magnet, drawing customers from across Western New York and Southern Ontario.

At the center stood AM&A's (Adam, Meldrum & Anderson Company). Founded in 1867 and operating until 1994, AM&A's was more than a store. It was an institution. Generations of Buffalonians marked holidays by its elaborate window displays, especially at Christmas, when downtown felt like a shared living room. Inside, shoppers found everything from fashion and

Above: Market Arcade Building. Opposite: 1950s- Looking south from Lafayette Square on Main Street

ACKERS
TOYS

furniture to housewares and toys, arranged across multiple floors with a sense of civic pride.

Nearby, Hengerer's catered to an upscale clientele, offering refined merchandise and attentive service before eventually being absorbed by Sibley's. L.L. Berger anchored the luxury end of the market, operating out of its landmark 1929 building at 514 Main Street and cultivating a reputation for elegance and exclusivity. Hens & Kelly rounded out the big players, reinforcing Main Street's role as a complete shopping ecosystem.

Not all retail was grand. Five-and-dime stores like Grant's and Kresge brought affordability and energy, their aisles buzzing with small purchases and big crowds. Specialty shops flourished alongside them. Kleinhan's dressed generations of Buffalo men, reinforcing the idea that downtown was where you went for quality and service.

Shopping hours reflected the rhythms of working life. Late-night Thursdays kept lights on and sidewalks busy well into the evening, turning retail into a social ritual. Downtown wasn't just functional; it was festive.

Suburban Shift and Decline (1960s–1980s)

The postwar decades brought forces that Main Street could not easily resist. Automobiles reshaped consumer behavior, and suburban growth redirected retail gravity outward. Shopping plazas and enclosed malls offered free parking, climate control, and proximity to new housing developments. Downtown, built for pedestrians and streetcars, struggled to compete.

The decision to construct the Buffalo Metro Rail in the late 1970s and early 1980s accelerated disruption. Main Street was transformed into a pedestrian mall during construction, severing automobile access and making already fragile retail even harder to reach. What was intended as a modern urban solution instead drained foot traffic at a critical moment.

At the same time, a deep recession hit Western New York. Manufacturing losses rippled through household budgets, and downtown

Top left: Hengerer's Department Store. Bottom right: Woolworth's lunch counter.

retail suffered a "tidal wave" of closures. Even stalwarts could not survive the combined pressure. The original Sears location at Main and Jefferson shut its doors, a symbolic blow to the idea that downtown remained the city's shopping heart. By the mid-1980s, vacant storefronts and darkened display windows became common sights.

Repurposing and Transformation *(1990s–Present)*

By the late 1990s, it became clear that downtown Buffalo would not return to its department-store past. The question shifted from restoration to reinvention. Vacant retail buildings, many architecturally significant, were repurposed into residential lofts, offices, and dining spaces. Upper floors that once held storage or unused apartments were reborn as living space, bringing residents back downtown for the first time in decades.

A critical milestone came in the 2010s with the restoration of automobile traffic to Main Street. The removal of the pedestrian mall reconnected neighborhoods, improved accessibility, and stitched together the Theatre District and Fountain Plaza. Retail did not return in its old form, but ground floors once again found purpose as cafés, restaurants, boutiques, and service-oriented businesses that catered to workers, residents, and visitors rather than regional shoppers.

Today's downtown retail is smaller in scale but more integrated into daily urban life. Instead of all-purpose department stores, Main Street offers curated experiences: dining before a show, coffee between meetings, specialty shopping tied to local identity. The emphasis is on reuse rather than replacement, on layering new activity into historic shells.

An Evolving Commercial Chalkboard

The history of downtown Buffalo retail is not a simple rise-and-fall story. It is a cycle of adaptation. From dry-goods shops with living quarters above, to grand department stores that turned shopping into spectacle, to a painful period of contraction, and finally to a mixed-use revival, Main Street has repeatedly rewritten its role.

What remains constant is its function as a mirror of Buffalo itself. When the city grew confident, retail expanded and dazzled. When the city struggled, storefronts went dark. And as Buffalo reimagines itself once again, downtown retail has shifted from being the city's shopping mall to being its shared front porch: smaller, more intimate, and rooted in place. The echoes of AM&A's holiday windows and late-night Thursdays still linger, not as blueprints to be replicated, but as reminders of how deeply commerce and civic life have always been intertwined on Main Street.

Top Left: AM&A's Chritmas Window
Bottom Right: Ice Skating at Fountain Plaza

A Short History of Buffalo's Colleges

Buffalo has always been a "make-it-work" town. It took marshland and river mouth and turned it into a port. It took grain, steel, smoke, snow, and stubbornness and turned them into a civic personality. So it makes perfect sense that Buffalo's colleges grew the same way: not as one clean "university town" plan, but as a practical, layered quilt stitched by churches, reformers, industrialists, immigrants, and public ambition. Higher education here didn't float down from the clouds. It arrived in boots, carrying a ledger, a Bible, a slide rule, and eventually a lab coat.

The city before the campus

In Buffalo's early decades, "college" wasn't a place so much as a promise. The city's growth in the nineteenth century was explosive, powered by canal commerce, Great Lakes shipping, and a fast-thickening web of industry. But growth creates appetite: for trained clergy and teachers, for lawyers and physicians, for engineers who could build the next bridge, the next terminal, the next set of waterworks, the next idea.

At first, that education often lived inside religious institutions and academies. Buffalo's immigrant communities built parishes and schools as quickly as they built homes. Those classrooms were the seedbeds of later colleges: disciplined learning, moral formation, and the social lift of literacy and credentials. If the grain elevators were Buffalo's vertical ambition, these early schools were its upward ladder.

Above: The original location of Canisius College on Washington Street. Opposite: Hayes Hall, University at Buffalo

Canisius: Jesuit rigor in a frontier city

One of the most enduring educational engines in Buffalo arrived with the Jesuits. Canisius College began in the 1870s, rooted in the Jesuit tradition of rigorous academics and public engagement. Its timing mattered. Buffalo was becoming a serious American city, and serious cities wanted serious institutions: places that could educate sons (and later daughters) of families who expected more than factory-floor fate.

Originally housed on Washington Street, Canisius wasn't built as a cloister. It grew in a city of arguments: labor and capital, old-stock and immigrant, Protestant and Catholic, machine politics and reform. Jesuit education thrives in the middle of that kind of friction, because it teaches students to reason, debate, write, and wrestle with ethical questions that aren't solved by slogans. In Buffalo, that meant graduates who could navigate the city's industrial complexity while keeping one eye on the moral math of power.

Buffalo State and the teacher-making mission

As the city expanded, the question wasn't only "Who will lead?" but "Who will teach the next wave?" New York State's normal schools, designed to train teachers, became critical civic infrastructure. Buffalo State's origins in teacher education reflect something important about

Rockwell Hall: The State University of New York Buffalo State University (colloquially referred to as simply Buff State)

Buffalo: this was a city that understood the long game. If you want a healthier workforce, a steadier democracy, and neighborhoods that don't fray at the seams, you invest in the people who stand at the front of the classroom every day.

Teacher training also helped professionalize education for women at a time when many fields still barred the door. In Buffalo, the path to influence often began with a chalkboard. That may not sound glamorous, but it's how cities get smarter: one lesson at a time, multiplied by decades.

UB: from local ambition to public powerhouse

If Buffalo's higher education story has a headline act, it's the University at Buffalo, now part of the State University of New York system. UB began as a private institution in the nineteenth century (a medical school was among its earliest roots) and evolved into a major public research university. That arc mirrors Buffalo's own identity shift: from merchant city to industrial titan to a modern metropolis re-tooling itself for the knowledge economy.

UB's growth wasn't just about adding buildings. It was about adding purpose. A research university changes the city around it. It attracts faculty and students from elsewhere, creates laboratories and clinics, generates patents and startups, and trains professionals who staff hospitals, law firms, engineering companies, and classrooms. In the twentieth century, as Buffalo navigated the rise and later decline of heavy industry, UB became part of the city's pivot: less smokestack, more brain-trust.

And then came the campuses themselves, which became a kind of geographical autobiography. UB's South Campus, woven into the city fabric, feels like an older Buffalo neighborhood: close, busy, human-scaled. The North Campus in Amherst, more expansive and modern, reflects postwar growth and suburban gravity. Together they tell a story many Buffalo families recognize in their own history: grandparents in the city, parents in the first ring, kids commuting between both worlds.

D'Youville, Trocaire, Medaille colleges with a mission

Not all Buffalo colleges were designed to be giant research machines. Some were designed to do something equally important: serve. Institutions like D'Youville (with its strong identity in health sciences), Trocaire, and Medaille developed around practical fields and community need, often with roots in religious or service traditions. Buffalo's strength has always been that it doesn't just build monuments; it builds institutions that show up for the daily work of care.

These schools trained nurses, therapists, educators, and social service professionals, the people who hold a city together when headlines move on. In Buffalo, healthcare and human services weren't abstract majors. They were neighborhood realities. A city with hard winters and hard work learns quickly that "helping professions" aren't soft. They're structural beams.

The medical corridor and the age of "knowledge industry"

By the late twentieth and early twenty-first centuries, Buffalo's colleges became central players in the city's economic reinvention. As factories closed and population declined, the question became: what replaces the old industrial base? Part of the answer came in the form of higher education linked to healthcare, biomedical research, and advanced manufacturing.

The Buffalo Niagara Medical Campus rose as a visible sign of this shift: a corridor where universities, hospitals, and research institutions cluster like a new kind of mill. Instead of ore and coal, the raw material is data, biology, and training. Instead of furnaces, there are imaging machines and wet labs. It's still Buffalo, though: still a place where people work with their hands and minds together, still a place where innovation is expected to prove itself in the real world.

Students now come to Buffalo not only for tradition but for opportunity: medical training, pharmacy, physical therapy, engineering, business, architecture, public health. The colleges have become both ladders for individuals and tools for the city's renewal.

Campus life as civic life

Buffalo's colleges have also been cultural engines. They bring lectures, performances, art shows, sports, and the constant churn of young people discovering who they are. In neighborhoods near campuses, you can feel the rhythm: coffee shops that refill faster in September, bookstores and buses and late-night diners that become unofficial classrooms. Even the city's arguments sharpen in the presence of students, because students ask "why" as a reflex.

And Buffalo benefits from that. A city can't live on nostalgia alone. Higher education keeps Buffalo in conversation with the wider world, importing new ideas and exporting graduates who carry Buffalo's DNA into other cities, then sometimes bring it back home.

What Buffalo's colleges reveal about Buffalo

If you stand back, Buffalo's college history reads like a civic self-portrait. It shows the city's religious diversity and its reform impulses. It shows the practical needs of an industrial economy and the later demands of a healthcare and research economy. It shows Buffalo's constant oscillation between city and suburb, between local roots and national reach. Most of all, it shows a stubborn commitment to upward motion.

Buffalo is often described through its infrastructure: canals, elevators, bridges, parks, power. But colleges are another kind of infrastructure, quieter and longer-lasting. They are human infrastructure. They take kids from South Buffalo and the East Side, from the first-ring suburbs and new immigrant families, and hand them tools: language, discipline, credentials, networks, a sense of possibility.

In a town that learned to build a harbor by observation and audacity, that's fitting. Buffalo's colleges are harbors too, in their own way. They catch talent. They shelter curiosity. They launch people into deeper water. And in a city where winter teaches endurance, the institutions that turn endurance into expertise may be the most Buffalo invention of all.

The former Olympic Theatre was located at 12 Broadway, the present site of the Rand Building.

Curtain Up!

The Buffalo Theatre District

The history of Buffalo's Theatre District is written in light and shadow, applause and silence, confidence and doubt. It follows the same arc as the city itself, rising with industrial wealth, faltering during economic retreat, and reemerging through persistence, imagination, and an unusual amount of civic courage. At its center stands Shea's Performing Arts Center, a building whose survival reshaped downtown Buffalo and, in many ways, altered how the city understands its own worth.

Early Stages: Entertainment Finds Main Street

By the late nineteenth century, Main Street had already established itself as Buffalo's primary commercial artery, and entertainment naturally followed commerce. Vaudeville houses, opera halls, and performance spaces clustered within walking distance of hotels, saloons, and department stores. Theatergoing was not a niche pastime. It was a central ritual of urban life, where working families, merchants, and elites shared the same seats, if not the same sections.

As the twentieth century opened, motion pictures joined live performance. Nickelodeons and early movie houses flourished, drawing steady crowds and reinforcing Main Street's role as a place where the city gathered after dark. Buffalo's growth fueled cultural ambition. Theaters grew larger, more ornate, and more confident, signaling that this was a city that expected to endure.

The Palace Era and the Birth of Shea's

That confidence found its grandest expression in 1926, when Shea's Buffalo Theatre opened its doors. Built as a movie and vaudeville palace, Shea's was unapologetically extravagant. Its scale, décor, and acoustics were designed to overwhelm, offering Depression-era audiences a brief escape into luxury and spectacle. For Buffalo, Shea's was not merely another venue; it was a statement of arrival.

For decades, Shea's anchored a dense constellation of theaters along Main Street. Broadway tours, films, concerts, and special events passed through the district, feeding nearby restaurants and shops. On show nights, downtown pulsed with energy. The Theatre District was not yet a branded concept, but it functioned as one, sustained by foot traffic, transit access, and habit.

Mid-Century Drift and Downtown Decline

After World War II, the district initially held steady. But subtle shifts soon compounded into structural change. Television altered how Americans spent their evenings. Suburbanization pulled residents away from downtown, along with retail and investment. As department stores shuttered and offices emptied after hours, the ecosystem that supported theaters weakened.

By the 1960s and 1970s, downtown Buffalo was visibly struggling. Urban renewal erased entire blocks. Main Street was reconfigured into a pedestrian mall during the construction of the Metro Rail, disrupting access and isolating businesses. Many theaters closed outright; others were subdivided, repurposed, or left to decay. The glow of marquees dimmed, replaced by boarded windows and uncertainty.

Shea's, despite its grandeur, was not immune. The vast building was expensive to maintain and increasingly out of step with prevailing entertainment economics. During this period, the theater fell into cycles of neglect and partial revival, mirroring downtown's broader instability.

Ownership Trouble and the Edge of Oblivion

In the 1960s and early 1970s, Shea's was owned by Leon Lawrence Sidell, who struggled to keep up with property taxes as downtown declined. The building slipped further into disrepair. Utilities were at risk. Deferred maintenance accumulated. Shea's survived, but just barely, sustained more by habit and hope than by financial logic.

The situation grew more precarious when Loew's Corporation pulled out, ending its involvement with the theater. Shea's passed into the hands of the City of Buffalo, raising uncomfortable questions. Could the city afford to maintain such a massive, aging structure? Did it even want to? For many decision-makers, the answers seemed obvious and grim.

The wheels were set in motion to demolish the landmark. Shea's, once a crown jewel, was now viewed by some as an obstacle to progress. All that remained was a signature authorizing payment for demolition.

That signature never came.

George O'Connell and the Moment That Mattered

At the decisive moment, Buffalo's comptroller, George O'Connell, intervened. Faced with an expense report to pay for demolition, O'Connell refused to sign off. His action was not dramatic in appearance, but it was monumental in consequence. By stopping the paperwork, he bought time. And in Buffalo's Theatre District, time proved to be everything.

Under O'Connell's watchful eye, Shea's utilities were kept running. The building did not go dark. Minimal repairs began. What had been framed as an inevitable loss became, once again, a question. And questions invite answers.

Soon after, Shea's was placed on the National Register of Historic Places, formalizing what many citizens already felt: that this was not just another building, but a cultural asset worth saving. Preservation now had legal standing as well as moral force.

The Friends, the Guild, and a City That Showed Up

With demolition halted, civic energy coalesced. The Shea's O'Connell Preservation Guild was formed to manage the theater and oversee its restoration. Around it grew a broader volunteer movement, often referred to as the Friends of Shea's or Friends of the Buffalo, made up of citizens who believed the city was better with the theater than without it.

This was not preservation by nostalgia alone. Volunteers scrubbed, painted, fundraised, and advocated. Government grants were pursued. A performance series was developed in the late 1970s to bring audiences back inside and generate revenue. The logic was simple but bold: the best way to save the theater was to use it.

The Queen City came together to save its crown. Donations arrived in small checks and large ones. Volunteers donated labor. Audiences returned, sometimes sitting in coats under temporary fixes, proving demand still existed. Shea's became a cause, a shared project that cut across neighborhoods and politics.

Over time, the volunteer-led Friends group gave way to a professional management team, reflecting the scale and seriousness of the undertaking. Restoration moved from survival mode to strategic renewal. Phase by phase, Shea's reclaimed its grandeur.

The Theatre District Reawakens

Shea's revival did not happen in isolation. Its success rippled outward, encouraging reinvestment in nearby venues and reinforcing the idea that Main Street could once again host nightlife. The loosely defined entertainment corridor began to reassemble itself into what is now formally recognized as the Theatre District.

Streetscape improvements, coordinated lighting, and signage reinforced identity. Restaurants and bars followed audiences back downtown. Hotels saw renewed demand. Importantly, the district began to operate as an ecosystem again, where a night at the theater meant dinner before, drinks after, and a reason to linger.

When automobile traffic returned to Main Street in the 2010s, accessibility improved further, stitching the Theatre District back into the larger downtown fabric. What had once been isolated pockets of activity became connected again.

Meaning Beyond the Marquee

The Buffalo Theatre District's history is not simply about entertainment. It is about values. At multiple moments, the city faced choices between erasure and continuity. Saving Shea's required believing that cultural infrastructure mattered as much as roads or office towers. It required patience when returns were uncertain and faith when demolition seemed easier.

The theater's repeated brushes with disrepair in the 1960s and 1970s underscore a deeper truth: decline is rarely sudden. It is cumulative. So is revival. Shea's survived not because it was perfect, but because enough people refused to accept its loss.

Today, when marquee lights glow along Main Street, they illuminate more than upcoming shows. They light a layered history of vaudeville acts, film premieres, civic neglect, near-destruction, and improbable rescue. Shea's stands as proof that cities are not only built by what they construct, but by what they choose not to tear down.

A District That Carries Memory Forward

The Theatre District now plays a central role in downtown Buffalo's daily life, drawing residents, visitors, and suburbanites back into the city core. It anchors hotels, complements retail, and provides shared experiences that no online substitute can replicate. Its success reinforces a lesson Buffalo has learned repeatedly: culture is not decorative. It is structural.

By saving Shea's, Buffalo preserved more than a theater. It preserved a sense of itself as a city worth the effort. The district endures because it does what it always has: gathers people together, holds them in collective attention, and sends them back out into the night reminded that their city, like its great theater, is still standing.

The Buffalo Niagara Medical Campus

From Industrial Hinterland to Innovation District

The Buffalo Niagara Medical Campus did not emerge overnight, nor was it the result of a single masterstroke. Instead, it grew deliberately, block by block, from a part of the city long defined by underused land, surface parking, and the quiet erosion that followed Buffalo's industrial decline. What stands there today is one of the region's most powerful economic engines: a dense, walkable concentration of healthcare, research, education, and biotech that has reshaped not only downtown's eastern edge, but Buffalo's sense of its own future.

The campus's roots reach back more than a century, anchored by Roswell Park Comprehensive Cancer Center, founded in 1898 as the nation's first institution dedicated exclusively to cancer research. Long before "innovation districts" became fashionable planning terms, Roswell Park was already drawing patients, clinicians, and scientists from around the world. Its global reputation provided both credibility and gravitational pull, quietly setting the stage for a broader medical ecosystem to form around it.

That ecosystem expanded steadily through the twentieth century, particularly with the presence of Buffalo General Medical Center, one of Western New York's largest and most important hospitals. As part of Kaleida Health, Buffalo General brought scale, clinical depth, and a constant flow of patients and professionals into the district. Together, Roswell Park and Buffalo General formed a medical anchor strong enough to support future growth, even during periods when downtown Buffalo struggled to retain momentum.

The modern concept of the Buffalo Niagara Medical Campus began to crystallize in the early 2000s, as civic leaders recognized that healthcare and life sciences offered a realistic path forward for a post-industrial city. Rather than isolating hospitals behind parking ramps and arterial roads, planners embraced density, connectivity, and urban integration. Streets were preserved. New buildings met sidewalks. The goal was not just medical excellence, but a living neighborhood where research, treatment, education, and daily life overlapped.

That vision gained dramatic momentum with the arrival of the Jacobs School of Medicine and Biomedical Sciences, which opened its downtown home in 2017. Moving the University at Buffalo's medical school from its long-established suburban South Campus into the heart of the city was both symbolic and practical. Students now train alongside clinicians at major hospitals, while faculty researchers collaborate across institutions without leaving the district. Just as importantly, the presence of hundreds of students injected daily foot traffic, energy, and demand for housing, food, and services into surrounding streets.

Clinical specialization further strengthened the campus with the opening of the Gates Vascular Institute, a facility designed to integrate advanced vascular surgery, imaging, and research under one roof. Connected physically and operationally to Buffalo General, Gates Vascular exemplifies the campus's emphasis on collaboration and efficiency. It also underscores how the BNMC is not merely a collection of hospitals, but an interconnected system designed to accelerate innovation while improving patient outcomes.

Pediatric care found its modern flagship in John R. Oishei Children's Hospital, which opened in 2017 as well. Consolidating children's services into a single, purpose-built facility, Oishei redefined family-centered care in the region. Its bright interiors, street-facing entrances, and integration with the surrounding neighborhood marked a sharp departure from the inward-looking hospital architecture of earlier generations. For many Buffalonians, Oishei became the most visible sign that the medical campus was not just growing, but evolving in how it related to the city around it.

Research remains a cornerstone of the campus's

identity, reinforced by institutions such as the Hauptman-Woodward Medical Research Institute. Internationally respected for its work in structural biology and crystallography, Hauptman-Woodward connects Buffalo directly to global scientific networks. Its presence highlights an often-overlooked truth about the BNMC: much of its impact happens quietly, in labs and offices where discoveries ripple outward long after headlines fade.

Beyond the marquee institutions, the campus has catalyzed a broader ecosystem. Startups, incubators, and support organizations cluster nearby, drawn by proximity to talent, funding, and clinical partners. Housing has followed, from adaptive reuse of older buildings to new construction aimed at students, professionals, and staff who want to live close to work. Cafés, restaurants, and small retailers now occupy ground floors that once sat dormant, giving the area a rhythm that extends beyond hospital shift changes.

The BNMC's influence is not purely economic, though its employment numbers are substantial. Tens of thousands of jobs are directly tied to campus institutions, with many more supported indirectly. Equally important is its role in stabilizing adjacent neighborhoods. Areas once written off as transitional or temporary have gained long-term residents and investment, reducing vacancy and reinforcing downtown's eastern corridor as a place to live as well as work.

Culturally, the medical campus represents a pivot point in Buffalo's self-image. It signals a shift from smokestacks and grain dust to labs, classrooms, and operating rooms without pretending the industrial past never existed. Many campus buildings rise on land once devoted to warehouses, rail spurs, or parking lots that replaced demolished factories. Adaptive reuse projects coexist with sleek new construction, creating a layered urban fabric rather than a tabula rasa.

The campus's planners made a deliberate choice to grow into the city rather than wall themselves off from it. Streets remain open. Blocks are walkable. Public art and streetscape improvements reinforce the sense that this is a shared district, not a gated enclave. In a city long shaped by single-use zones, the BNMC stands as a counterexample: dense, mixed, and interconnected.

In practical terms, the Buffalo Niagara Medical Campus has helped anchor downtown during periods of uncertainty, providing stability when other sectors faltered. In symbolic terms, it offers proof that Buffalo can build a future rooted in knowledge, care, and discovery while remaining true to its urban DNA. Where industry once defined progress, healing and research now do the work of shaping the city's next chapter.

When Buffalo Gathers

Festivals as Civic Ritual

Buffalo is a city that understands winter, loss, and patience. It is also a city that understands release. When the weather breaks and the streets reopen, Buffalo does not merely host festivals. It practices them. These gatherings are not ornamental add-ons to civic life. They are how the city remembers itself, negotiates difference, and reasserts joy in public.

Taken together, Buffalo's festivals form a calendar of belonging. Each one reflects a different neighborhood, history, or cultural current, yet all share a common trait: they spill outward. Streets close. Parks fill. Private traditions become public invitations.

Art, Music, and the Start of Summer

For many, the seasonal turning point is the Allentown Art Festival. Since 1957, it has transformed Delaware Avenue into a long, open-air gallery. Fine art lines a boulevard originally built to impress, temporarily flattening the distance between collectors and casual strollers. The setting matters. The Allentown neighborhood's historic bohemian streak gives the festival a tone that is confident but unpretentious. It is art without velvet ropes, signaling that culture in Buffalo is something you walk into, not around.

That openness carries directly into sound. Music Is Art, founded by Robby Takac of the Goo Goo Dolls, celebrates Buffalo's musical ecosystem with deliberate inclusivity. Genres overlap. Established acts share stages with emerging ones. The festival's name is less slogan than statement: creativity here is not siloed. Music Is Art reflects a city comfortable with hybridity, where polish and grit coexist.

Above: Allentown Art Festival Opposite: Dyngus Day Parade

BROADWAY Market
BROADWAY SEAFOOD
SPEED LIMIT
30

Taste of Buffalo

Food as Identity

If art and music open the season, food anchors it. The Taste of Buffalo turns downtown into a collective table. One of the largest two-day food festivals in the country, it condenses Buffalo's restaurant scene into bite-sized declarations of pride. Lines stretch across Niagara Square. Old favorites and newer ventures stand shoulder to shoulder. Everyone eats the same way: standing, comparing, recommending. Taste of Buffalo is democratic by design. It reminds the city that its culinary identity is not a trend, but an inheritance continually renewed.

Ethnic festivals deepen that inheritance. Buffalo's Greek and Italian celebrations turn food into living history. The Greek Festival of Buffalo, long hosted by Holy Trinity Greek Orthodox Church, blends music, dance, and cuisine into an expression of continuity. Likewise, the Italian Festival on Hertel Avenue transforms a neighborhood corridor into a shared memory lane, where immigration stories are told through recipes, songs, and family ritual rather than speeches.

Faith, Folklore, and Humor

Some Buffalo festivals are best understood through temperament. Dyngus Day arrives the Monday after Easter with pussy willows, polka, and a collective wink. Rooted in Polish tradition, Dyngus Day embraces absurdity as cultural glue. Participants spray water, dance in the streets, and wear their heritage lightly but proudly. In a city often portrayed as stoic, Dyngus Day insists that humor is also tradition.

Irish identity surfaces with similar multiplicity. Buffalo hosts not one but two major St. Patrick's Day parades, each reflecting a different strand of the city's Irish story. The Delaware Avenue parade projects scale and visibility, a broad civic procession that draws crowds from across the region. The Old Neighborhood parade in South Buffalo offers something more intimate. It is community-forward, rooted in the streets where Irish families built lives along the waterfront. Together, the two parades tell a fuller story: assimilation and persistence, spectacle and memory, both necessary.

Memory, Justice, and Celebration

Some festivals carry heavier weight without losing joy. Juneteenth Festival at Martin Luther King Jr. Park is among the city's most significant gatherings. One of the longest-running and largest Juneteenth celebrations in the nation, it blends remembrance with affirmation. Music, food, education, and parade converge in a space long central to Buffalo's Black community. Juneteenth insists that history be acknowledged publicly, not quietly footnoted. It also insists that freedom, once named, must be celebrated out loud.

Music carries that insistence forward at the Pine Grill Jazz Reunion, a free, annual festival honoring Buffalo's jazz era of the 1950s and 1960s. Held at MLK Park, the reunion channels a time when Jefferson Avenue clubs pulsed nightly with local and national talent. The festival is less about nostalgia than continuity. Veteran musicians share space with younger players. The audience listens on blankets and folding chairs. Jazz, once played in tight rooms, opens itself to the sky.

What These Festivals Do

Individually, Buffalo's festivals are entertaining. Collectively, they perform civic work. They collapse distance between neighborhoods. They bring suburban visitors into city streets without apology. They allow newcomers to step inside traditions rather than observe from the edge.

They also recalibrate public space. Streets built for cars become places for conversation. Parks designed for pass-through become destinations. The city temporarily rearranges itself around people rather than efficiency. That rearrangement leaves residue. Once you have danced on a boulevard or eaten in a square, you see the city differently afterward.

Equally important is durability. Many of these festivals have lasted decades. They survived recessions, population loss, and shifting tastes. Their endurance signals trust. People return because these events deliver something reliable: recognition. You will see someone you know. You will hear something familiar. You will belong without explanation.

A City That Knows How to Show Up

Buffalo's festivals do not pretend to solve the city's problems. They do something quieter and arguably more essential. They keep civic muscle exercised. They remind residents how to occupy space together. They rehearse belonging.

In a place shaped by industry, weather, and reinvention, festivals are how Buffalo practices optimism without denying history. They allow joy to coexist with memory, humor with hardship, and pride with openness.

When Buffalo gathers like this, it is not performing for outsiders. It is talking to itself, out loud, in streets and parks that remember.

Pride Parade

The Buffalo & Erie County Naval Park

Steel, Sacrifice, and a Waterfront That Remembers

Moored along the edge of Buffalo's Inner Harbor, the Buffalo and Erie County Naval & Military Park is impossible to miss and difficult to forget. Gray hulls rise from the water where freighters once queued, their silhouettes both martial and contemplative. This is not a monument set apart from daily life. It is a living presence on the waterfront, a place where history rests at the waterline and quietly insists on being acknowledged.

A Natural Harbor for Memory

Buffalo's connection to the military predates the park by centuries. Its strategic location at the eastern edge of Lake Erie made it a gateway during the War of 1812 and later a critical industrial contributor during both World Wars. Steel, grain, munitions, and manufactured goods flowed through the harbor to support national defense. When peace returned, the city carried the imprint of those efforts in its workforce and waterfront.

The idea of a naval park emerged during the Cold War era, when decommissioned ships faced scrap yards or distant memorials. Buffalo recognized an opportunity. By anchoring vessels here, the city could honor service, educate the public, and repurpose its waterfront at a moment when traditional maritime industry was fading. The harbor that once supplied war would now preserve its memory.

The Naval Park officially opened in the late 1970s, aligning with broader efforts to reimagine Buffalo's waterfront. The choice was deliberate. Rather than placing military artifacts inland or behind museum walls, Buffalo kept them afloat, where water, weather, and scale reinforced their original context.

Ships With Stories

At the heart of the park are its ships, each representing a different era and function of naval warfare. The guided missile cruiser USS Little Rock serves as the park's centerpiece. Commissioned in 1945 and later converted into a guided missile cruiser during the Cold War, Little Rock reflects the transition from World War II conventional warfare to the missile age. Its decks and compartments reveal how technology reshaped naval life, from radar rooms to command centers designed for global tension rather than fleet engagement.

Nearby rests the destroyer USS The Sullivans, a ship whose story carries extraordinary emotional weight. Named for the five Sullivan brothers from Waterloo, Iowa, who were killed together aboard the USS Juneau during World War II, The Sullivans embodies sacrifice at its most personal. The ship saw extensive service in the Pacific Theater and later during the Korean War. Walking its narrow passageways brings visitors face to face with the human scale of war, where courage coexisted with cramped quarters and constant risk.

Also part of the collection is the cruiser USS Croaker, a World War II submarine that adds a submerged dimension to the park's narrative. Croaker represents the unseen side of naval warfare, where stealth, endurance, and isolation defined missions. Descending into its interior, visitors experience the claustrophobic conditions submariners endured for weeks at a time, a sharp contrast to the open decks above.

Together, these vessels form a layered story of twentieth-century conflict, technological evolution, and service. They are not replicas or abstractions. They are working ships retired with their histories intact.

246

E

More Than Hardware

While ships draw the eye, the Naval Park's purpose extends beyond steel and rivets. The site functions as an educational space, interpreting military history through personal experience. Exhibits highlight life aboard ship, naval hierarchy, and the global contexts in which these vessels operated. Veterans often serve as guides, adding firsthand perspective that no placard can replace.

The park also honors branches beyond the Navy. Memorials and installations recognize Marines, soldiers, airmen, and Coast Guard members, reinforcing the idea that national defense is collective. Names etched in stone coexist with interactive exhibits, blending solemnity with engagement. The Battle Within Memorial serves both those that have lost their lives to PTSD and those who are currently suffering. Photos of those who have passed, attached by magnets, are a poignet reminder of this ongoing issue.

Anchored in the City

What makes the Naval Park distinctive is its relationship to Buffalo itself. The ships sit within sight of downtown offices, Canalside events, and waterfront promenades. Concertgoers, office workers, and tourists pass by daily. This proximity normalizes remembrance. Military history is not confined to anniversaries or ceremonies. It becomes part of the everyday visual landscape.

Winter adds another dimension. Snow gathers on decks. Ice forms along the hulls. The ships look resolute and vulnerable at once, echoing the endurance of the city that shelters them. Few naval parks operate year-round in such conditions, and that persistence underscores Buffalo's commitment to keeping the site alive rather than ornamental.

Veterans and Civic Life

The Naval Park serves as a gathering place for veterans' ceremonies, school visits, and public observances. Memorial Day and Veterans Day events draw crowds that bridge generations. For older veterans, the ships offer recognition. For younger visitors, they offer context. The park functions as a translator between lived experience and historical understanding.

Importantly, the site does not glorify war uncritically. Its tone is reflective rather than triumphant. Displays acknowledge loss alongside service. Visitors are encouraged to consider not only battles won, but lives altered. This balance aligns with Buffalo's broader civic character, shaped by labor, sacrifice, and resilience rather than spectacle.

A Waterfront Reclaimed

The Naval Park also played a quiet role in Buffalo's waterfront revival. Long before Canalside became a destination, the ships provided a reason to come to the water. They established presence and purpose when much of the Inner Harbor was still underused. In that sense, the park functioned as a bridge between the waterfront's industrial past and its public future.

As surrounding development expanded, the Naval Park remained constant. It adapted through maintenance, restoration, and expanded programming, but its core mission did not shift. The ships stayed put, anchoring change around them.

A Floating Archive

Ultimately, the Buffalo & Erie County Naval Park is a floating archive. It preserves not just machines, but memory. It tells a story about service, technology, and national effort, while also telling a local story about a city that chose remembrance over removal.

Buffalo once sent ships, steel, and labor outward to support war. Today, it welcomes those ships home and offers them a place to rest. Along the harbor where commerce once ruled, the Naval Park asks a quieter question: not how much a city can move, but how well it remembers.

43North and the Spark of Buffalo's Startup Economy

When Buffalo speaks about reinvention in the twenty-first century, 43North stands near the center of the conversation. They were launched in 2014 as part of New York State's Buffalo Billion initiative. The program set out to do something both simple and bold: attract high-growth startups to Buffalo, provide them with seed-stage funding to scale their company and prove that a city once defined by steel and grain could also compete in software, biotech, consumer packaged goods, and emerging industries.

At its core, 43North is an annual startup competition. Each year, hundreds, sometimes thousands, of companies from around the world apply. A select cohort is chosen to receive significant prize funding, along with office space, mentorship, and access to a growing network of investors and partners.

Raising capital in exchange for equity is standard for early-stage founders. What differentiated 43North was that the investment came with a commitment on both sides: companies relocated to Buffalo, and in return gained hands-on support, access to customers and investors, and a city willing to rally behind high-growth businesses. It made clear that Buffalo wasn't chasing a moment—it was committing to entrepreneurs for the long term

Early skepticism was natural. Could startups built for global markets truly thrive in a mid-sized Rust Belt city better known for lake-effect snow than venture capital? A decade later, the results are measured but substantial. 43North companies have created more than a thousand jobs locally and roughly 3,000 globally. They have raised significant follow-on capital, attracted national attention, and helped establish Buffalo as a credible player in the innovation economy. While unicorns remain rare everywhere, companies emerging from 43North's portfolio have achieved IPOs and billion-dollar valuations, proving that high-growth potential is not confined to coastal zip codes.

Geography has played an important role in that shift. Many 43North portfolio companies are located in reimagined towers like Seneca One or near the Buffalo Niagara Medical Campus. Their presence brought a new rhythm to the city center. Coffee shops filled with laptops. Networking events replaced vacant lobbies. Flexible workspaces hum with experimentation. These changes may seem incremental, but collectively they have reshaped expectations about what downtown Buffalo can be.

Importantly, 43North did not operate in isolation. It intersected with broader developments, including the growth of the Buffalo Niagara Medical Campus, university research commercialization, and increased interest in downtown living. Health technology, fintech, logistics, and SaaS firms found synergy with regional strengths in healthcare, education, manufacturing, and cross-border trade. In this sense, 43North acted as a catalyst, accelerating existing assets rather than attempting to replace them.

That catalytic effect is visible in complementary institutions such as the Northland Workforce Training Center. Designed as an industry-driven public-private partnership, Northland focuses on closing the skills gap in advanced manufacturing and energy sectors. By addressing barriers like transportation, childcare, academic readiness, and affordability, it creates economic on-ramps for Western New Yorkers seeking stable, high-paying careers. Together, entrepreneurial acceleration and workforce development represent two sides of Buffalo's reinvention strategy: innovation at the top and opportunity across the base.

Perhaps 43North's most significant contribution has been narrative. For decades, Buffalo was framed through loss–lost industry, lost population, lost relevance. The startup competition helped reframe that story. Founders from California, Europe, and beyond began coming to Buffalo not out of nostalgia, but because it made business sense. Headlines shifted from decline to possibility.

43North has not singlehandedly transformed Buffalo's economy, nor was it intended to. Its lasting impact lies in proof of concept. It demonstrated that capital, talent, and ambition can thrive in an old industrial city with strong foundations. In doing so, it reinforced a familiar lesson: Buffalo's resilience is not accidental.
It adapts, experiments, and builds again–this time, one startup at a time.

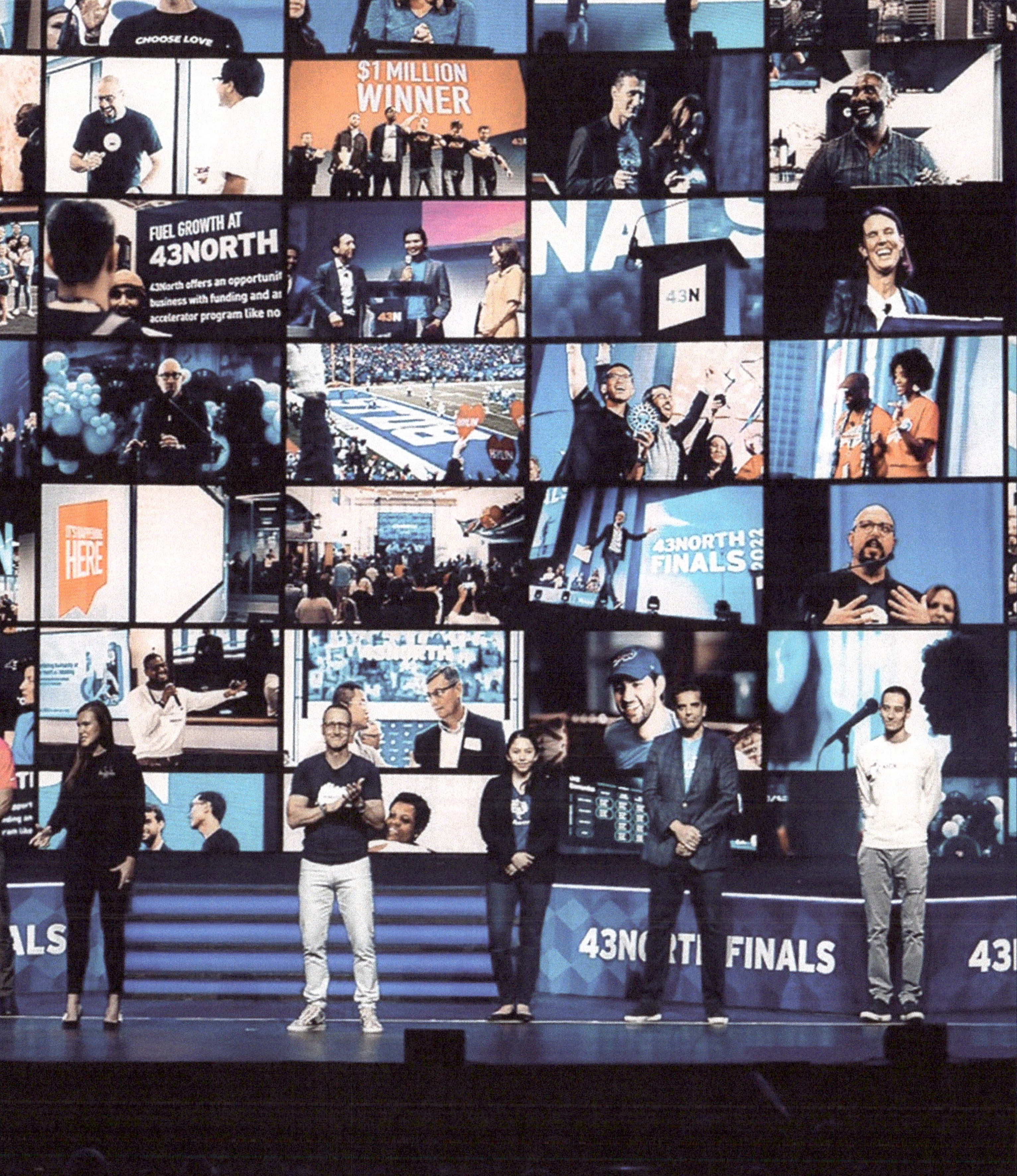

CHOOSE LOVE
$1 MILLION WINNER
FUEL GROWTH AT
43NORTH
43N
43N
IT'S HAPPENING HERE
43NORTH FINALS 2022
FINALS

The City That Shows Up

Buffalo has a habit of showing up. Not loudly. Not performatively. Just steadily, like a neighbor knocking with a shovel in hand before you even think to ask. In a place where winter can rearrange your roofline overnight and lake effect snow writes its own weather reports, mutual aid is not a slogan. It is choreography.

When storms roll in off Lake Erie and bury cars like forgotten toys, the ritual begins. Strangers dig out strangers. Snowblowers hum in relay formation down city blocks. Church basements become warming centers. Volunteers fan out with hot coffee and casseroles. During blizzards, social media transforms into a digital command center, matching those who need help with those who have muscle and time. Buffalo does not wait for rescue. It becomes rescue.

That reflex extends well beyond winter.

Rebuilding with Purpose

Buffalo ReUse rescues doors, windows, fixtures, and architectural fragments from demolition and gives them second lives. What might have become landfill instead becomes possibility. Salvaged materials are sold affordably, keeping historic character intact while offering job training and community workshops. In a city defined by sturdy buildings and second chances, reuse is both environmental ethic and civic metaphor.

Grassroots Gardens WNY tends a different kind of restoration. Across vacant lots and neighborhood corners, raised beds bloom where asphalt once dominated. Residents grow vegetables, herbs, and friendships in the same soil. These gardens provide fresh food, yes, but they also cultivate agency. Neighbors plan together, plant together, and harvest together. In the process, blocks feel safer, more connected, more alive.

On Buffalo's West Side, Massachusetts Avenue Project expands that work through urban farming and youth development. Its farm on the city's West Side trains young people in food systems, leadership, and entrepreneurship. Teens cultivate produce that supplies neighborhood markets while learning how food justice connects to economic justice. Rows of kale and peppers double as classrooms. The harvest is tangible, but so is the confidence that grows alongside it.

Housing stability is another pillar of lift. PUSH Buffalo, short for People United for Sustainable Housing, organizes residents to create affordable housing, advocate for energy efficiency, and

PUSH Buffalo – helps to create strong neighborhoods with quality, affordable housing;

Grassroots Community Gardens

advance equitable development. PUSH renovates homes, supports first time homeowners, and pushes policy conversations toward fairness. In neighborhoods long overlooked, it turns disinvestment into reinvestment. Walls are repaired, porches rebuilt, and families remain rooted rather than displaced. Stability, here, is not abstract. It has an address.

Water, the city's original engine, has its guardians too. For thirty five years, Buffalo Niagara Waterkeeper has worked as steward of Western New York's freshwater systems. River cleanups, habitat restoration, policy advocacy, and youth education programs all flow from a single premise: clean water is not a luxury but a birthright. By protecting Lake Erie and the Buffalo River, Waterkeeper protects public health, recreation, and the ecological backbone of the region.

Feeding with Dignity

Hunger, unlike snow, does not announce itself in drifts. It hides in cupboards and quiet worry. In response, FeedMore WNY unites what were once The Food Bank of WNY and Meals on Wheels for WNY under one mission: to feed more Western New Yorkers of all ages for whom securing nutritious food is a challenge. The goal is contained in the name. The mission is larger. FeedMore WNY offers dignity, hope, and a brighter future through nutritious food, friendship, and skills training. Volunteers sort donations in warehouses. Drivers deliver meals to homebound seniors. Nutrition programs teach families how to stretch ingredients into healthy dinners.

The Salvation Army of Buffalo layers additional support. Its food pantries, clothing distribution, hygiene products, and emergency financial assistance address immediate crises. Emergency family shelters and rapid re housing programs offer stability. Through Pathway of Hope case management, after school programs, music instruction, GED classes, and employment counseling, the organization tackles cycles of

Feedmore WNY helps to fill food pantry's

poverty from multiple angles. Seasonal initiatives supply winter coats, back to school essentials, and holiday toys.

On the city's West Side, West Side Community Services strengthens stability by engaging and connecting residents through family support and youth programming grounded in inclusion and belonging.

At street level, compassion is even more direct. Friends of Night People serves hot meals, distributes clothing, and provides medical care to those experiencing homelessness. Harvest House provides meals and essential supplies to individuals facing food insecurity with unwavering consistency.

Healing in Motion

Care also travels by foot. UB HEALS, a student run street medicine team from the University at Buffalo Jacobs School of Medicine and Biomedical Sciences, brings healthcare directly to shelters and encampments. Since 2016, volunteers have delivered basic medical care, supplies, and referrals every Tuesday and Thursday, bridging gaps in access for people who might otherwise go untreated. It trains future physicians to see medicine not only as clinical practice, but as civic responsibility.

A Culture of Lift

What links snow shovels, garden beds, housing rehabilitation, meal deliveries, river cleanups, and street medicine rounds is not coincidence. It is culture. Buffalo residents and organizations operate with a shared understanding that resilience is collective. The city's history includes economic upheaval, blizzards, industrial loss, and reinvention. Through it all, neighbors have learned that survival improves when shared.

In Buffalo, lifting people up is not charity performed at a distance. It is proximity. It is a volunteer knee deep in river mud pulling debris from the current. It is a student checking blood pressure beneath an overpass. It is a carpenter salvaging a century old door so another home can stay whole. It is a block of houses clearing a path before the plow arrives.

The skyline may announce industry and architecture. The true architecture of Buffalo, however, is relational. Beam by beam, act by act, the city constructs a structure of care sturdy enough to withstand weather, want, and time.

OBX

Canalside and the Outer Harbor

Full-Circle: The Future is Right Where We Began

For much of its history, Buffalo's waterfront was a place you worked, not a place you lingered. It was loud, dangerous, and essential. Grain dust hung in the air, ships crowded the slips, and the edge between land and water was measured in profit and peril. That reality shaped the city for more than a century. The story of Canalside and the Outer Harbor is the story of how Buffalo chose to reinterpret that inheritance, not by erasing it, but by opening it to the public.

Rediscovering the Inner Harbor

The idea behind Canalside was deceptively simple: return people to the place where Buffalo began. But doing so required decades of planning, debate, and incremental progress. Archaeology preceded design. Historians and planners worked to interpret the original Erie Canal Harbor in a way that balanced accuracy with usability.

When Canalside finally emerged in the early twenty-first century, it was not a museum in the traditional sense. Instead, it functioned as a living public space layered with history. Recreated canal outlines trace where water once flowed. Interpretive elements coexist with lawns, docks, and promenades. Kayaks now move through spaces once choked with cargo.

Canalside reintroduced Buffalonians to their waterfront gradually. Concerts, festivals, ice skating, and casual gatherings built familiarity. The goal was not spectacle alone, but habit. By giving residents reasons to return repeatedly, the city rebuilt a relationship that had been severed for generations.

Opposite: Canalside - Central Wharf

A Civic Front Porch

Today, Canalside operates as Buffalo's civic front porch. It hosts large events, but it also accommodates ordinary afternoons. Office workers eat lunch by the water. Families wander without agenda. Visitors encounter the city's origin story without needing a guidebook.

Crucially, Canalside reconnected downtown to Lake Erie. Visual and physical access mattered. Water once hidden behind infrastructure became visible again. The shoreline shifted from boundary to invitation. That shift altered how Buffalo understood itself. The city was no longer oriented solely inward, toward land-based industry, but outward, toward the water that made it possible.

Beyond the Inner Harbor: The Outer Harbor Emerges

If Canalside represents reclamation, the Outer Harbor represents expansion. Stretching south and west of downtown, the Outer Harbor encompasses hundreds of acres of former industrial land, breakwalls, and open water. For decades, this space was largely inaccessible, known more to fishermen and urban explorers than to the general public.

As industry retreated, opportunity emerged. The question was scale. Should the Outer Harbor become an extension of downtown, densely developed and programmed? Or should it remain open, natural, and flexible? Buffalo's answer has leaned deliberately toward openness.

Trails, kayak launches, small beaches, and informal gathering spots appeared first. Nature reclaimed ground once covered by concrete. Wildflowers, birds, and grasses returned. The Outer Harbor became a place for walking, cycling, and quiet observation, offering a counterpoint to the activity at Canalside.

A New Kind of Park

That philosophy reached a milestone with the development of Ralph Wilson Park, a transformative project along the lake. Designed as a world-class waterfront park, it prioritizes ecological restoration, access, and scale. Sweeping lawns, elevated landforms, and restored shoreline create a space that feels expansive rather than programmed to exhaustion.

Ralph Wilson Park signals a shift in how Buffalo thinks about its waterfront future. Instead of asking how much can be built, the city asked how much could be given back. The result is a landscape that invites reflection as much as recreation, aligning with contemporary values around sustainability and public health.

From Cargo to Culture

Cultural reuse has also played a role. Historic structures and former port facilities have found new life as event spaces and destinations, reinforcing continuity between past and present. While Canalside interprets history explicitly, the Outer Harbor allows it to linger implicitly, in the bones of breakwalls and the geometry of slips that still shape the shoreline.

Events at the waterfront now range from large concerts to small community gatherings. The water has become a stage, but one that does not require constant amplification. Sometimes the most meaningful experiences are quiet: a sunset over the lake, a freighter passing on the horizon, the wind moving across open grass.

A Shift in Civic Identity

Together, Canalside and the Outer Harbor represent one of Buffalo's most profound civic transformations. They mark a shift from exclusion to access, from utility to experience. Importantly, they also mark a psychological change. For generations, Buffalo's waterfront symbolized loss: lost industry, lost jobs, lost relevance. Reclaiming it reframed that narrative.

This transformation did not erase history. Grain elevators still loom nearby. Harbor infrastructure remains visible. The difference is agency. Buffalo now chooses how the water is used, rather than being dictated to by global shipping markets alone.

An Incomplete, Ongoing Project

The waterfront's story is not finished. Development pressures persist. Balancing access, preservation, and growth will remain a challenge. But the framework is established. Public space comes first. Water is shared, not hidden. History is acknowledged, not buried.

That balance matters. Canalside thrives because it is active. The Outer Harbor thrives because it is spacious. Together, they offer complementary experiences that reflect Buffalo's complexity.

Where the City Breathes

In the end, Canalside and the Outer Harbor are not just redevelopment projects. They are statements about what kind of city Buffalo wants to be. They say that public space matters. That history can be touched. That water belongs to everyone.

Once, Buffalo turned its back on the lake that made it. Today, the city faces it again, openly. In doing so, it has reclaimed not only its shoreline, but a sense of possibility that flows, like the canal once did, outward to the world.

Opposite: Concert at Terminal B

What Endures

Cities like Buffalo are often measured by what they build and what they lose. Grain elevators rise and fall. Factories roar, then go silent. Neighborhoods swell with newcomers, thin with departures, and quietly reinvent themselves again. From a distance, history can look like a sequence of booms and busts, fortunes made and squandered. Up close, however, Buffalo's story has always been less about cycles and more about continuity.

What endures here is not a single industry, ethnicity, or era, but a habit of adaptation. From the Seneca Nation's deep relationship with land and water, to frontier settlers carving a harbor from mud and ice, to immigrants who arrived with little more than muscle and memory, Buffalo has repeatedly absorbed disruption and turned it into structure. Loss was rarely the end of the story. It was information. It taught the city how to rebuild smarter, tougher, and with a longer view.

The waterfront tells this story better than any monument. Once a place of backbreaking labor and lethal risk, it now hosts kayaks, concerts, and quiet paths through reclaimed grassland. Times Beach, Canalside, and the Outer Harbor are not triumphalist spaces. They are reflective ones. They acknowledge what was sacrificed, what was polluted, what was erased, and what–given time and restraint–could return. Renewal here did not come from pretending the past never happened. It came from listening to it.

Buffalo's neighborhoods carry the same lesson. The Old First Ward, the East Side, Black Rock, and Broadway-Fillmore were shaped by Irish, German, Polish, Italian, Jewish, and Black communities who built institutions because no one else would build them for them. Churches doubled as schools. Taverns became hiring halls and union headquarters. Markets turned into social centers where language, faith, and food braided together.

Even in moments of exclusion–whether through nativism, economic collapse, or organized hatred–those networks proved stronger than the forces arrayed against them.

The city's brush with darker movements, including the Ku Klux Klan, underscores this point. Intolerance did not disappear Buffalo. It was confronted, exposed, and rejected by civic leadership, organized labor, and ordinary citizens unwilling to let fear define their home. That resistance is as much a part of Buffalo's inheritance as any building or boulevard.

Today, Buffalo stands at another inflection point. The economy has shifted again. The waterfront has softened. Old structures have found new uses. The temptation, as always, is to declare a final version of the city: reborn, redeemed, finished. History suggests otherwise. Buffalo has never been finished. Its strength lies in motion, not arrival.

This book has traced water, labor, culture, conflict, and resilience across generations. What ties those threads together is not nostalgia, but recognition. Buffalo's future will not be built by abandoning its past, nor by embalming it. It will be shaped, as it always has been, by people willing to do unglamorous work, form durable communities, and make long bets on a place others once wrote off.

Buffalo endures because it remembers-and because it keeps going.

LOVE

About the Author

Mark Donnelly, PhD., is a former marketing professor, history geek, photographer, and creative instigator with more than 60 books to his name. He is best known as the graybeard lecturer who turned a squeaky whiteboard and an alarming intake of coffee into a teaching philosophy built on clarity, curiosity, and retelling the human experience.

Dr. Donnelly shaped his reputation the old-fashioned way: by simplifying the truth. Not the buzzword-heavy, corporate-approved version, but the real kind that only emerges after watching trends rise, fall, and reappear wearing different shoes. His work is grounded in the belief that complexity is often a failure of explanation, not intelligence, and that understanding should feel empowering, not exclusive.

Throughout academia, Donnelly also wandered productively through newspapers, publishing, consulting, community development, and philanthropic strategy. Along the way, he collected stories, scars, insights, and more thrift-store books than any one man reasonably needs. That varied path informs his teaching and writing style: part historian, part storyteller, part field guide for navigating change without losing your footing.

As a writer, Donnelly moves easily between disciplines, connecting marketing to neuroscience, history to culture, and cities to the people who build them. His historical work, particularly on Buffalo and Western New York, reflects the same sensibility as his teaching: respect for lived experience, skepticism of easy narratives, and deep interest in how people adapt when the ground shifts beneath them.

He lives and creates in Kenmore, New York, with his bride, Princess Laura, surrounded by an ever-growing pile of notebooks, half-finished ideas, and books he swears he's going to write next.

His lifelong principle remains simple: Make a difference.

This book is his latest attempt to do exactly that.

www.ingramcontent.com/pod-product-compliance
Lightning Source LLC
LaVergne TN
LVHW060601110826
845154LV00004B/107

* 9 7 8 1 9 5 6 6 8 8 6 9 6 *